لله الرحمن الرحيم

PERISHED
NATIONS

To The Reader

In all the books by the author, faith-related issues are explained in the light of Qur'anic verses, and people are invited to learn Allah's words and to live by them. All the subjects that concern Allah's verses are explained in such a way as to leave no room for doubt or question marks in the reader's mind. The sincere, plain and fluent style employed ensures that everyone of every age and from every social group can easily understand the books. This effective and lucid narrative makes it possible to read them in a single sitting. Even those who rigorously reject spirituality are influenced by the facts recounted in these books and cannot refute the truthfulness of their contents.

This book and all the other works by Harun Yahya can be read individually or discussed in a group. Those readers who are willing to profit from the books will find discussion very useful in that they will be able to relate their own reflections and experiences to one another.

In addition, it is a great service to the religion to contribute to the presentation and circulation of these books, which are written solely for the good pleasure of Allah. All the books of the author are extremely convincing, so, for those who want to communicate the religion to other people, one of the most effective methods is to encourage them to read these books.

It is hoped that the reader will take time to look through the review of other books on the final pages of the book, and appreciate the rich source of material on faith-related issues, which are very useful and a pleasure to read.

In them, one will not find, as in some other books, the personal views of the author, explanations based on dubious sources, styles unobservant of the respect and reverence due to sacred subjects, or hopeless, doubt-creating, and pessimistic accounts that create deviations in the heart.

PERISHED NATIONS

HARUN YAHYA

About The Author

The author, who writes under the pen-name HARUN YAHYA, was born in Ankara in 1956. Having completed his primary and secondary education in Ankara, he then studied arts at Istanbul's Mimar Sinan University and philosophy at Istanbul University. Since the 1980s, the author has published many books on political, faith-related and scientific issues. Harun Yahya is well-known as an author who has written very important works disclosing the imposture of evolutionists, the invalidity of their claims and the dark liaisons between Darwinism and bloody ideologies such as fascism and communism.

His pen-name is made up of the names "Harun" (Aaron) and "Yahya" (John), in memory of the two esteemed prophets who fought against lack of faith. The Prophet's seal on the cover of the books is symbolic and is linked to the their contents. It symbolises that the Qur'an is the final scripture and the Prophet Muhammad is the last of the prophets. Under the guidance of the Qur'an and sunnah, the author makes it his purpose to disprove each one of the fundamental tenets of godless ideologies and to have the "last word", so as to completely silence the objections raised against religion. The seal of the final Prophet, who attained ultimate wisdom and moral perfection, is used as a sign of his intention of saying this last word.

All author's works center around one goal: to convey the Qur'an's message to people, encourage them to think about basic faith-related issues (such as the existence of Allah, His unity and the Hereafter), and to expose the feeble foundations and perverted ideologies of godless systems.

Harun Yahya enjoys a wide readership in many countries, from India to America, England to Indonesia, Poland to Bosnia, and Spain to Brazil. Some of his books are available in English, French, German, Spanish, Italian, Portuguese, Urdu, Arabic, Albanian, Russian, Serbo-Croat (Bosnian), Polish, Malay, Uygur Turkish, and Indonesian, and they are enjoyed by readers world-wide.

Greatly appreciated all around the world, these works have been instrumental in many people recovering their faith in Allah and in many others gaining a deeper insight into their faith. The wisdom, and the sincere and easy-to-understand style gives these books a distinct touch which directly effects any one who reads or studies them. Immune to objections, these works are characterized by their features of rapid effectiveness, definite results and irrefutability. It is unlikely that those who read these books and give serious thought to them can any longer sincerely advocate the materialistic philosophy, atheism or any other perverted ideology or philosophy. Even if they continue to do so, it will be only a sentimental insistence since these books refuted such ideologies from their very foundations. All contemporary movements of denial are now ideologically defeated, thanks to the collection of books written by Harun Yahya.

There is no doubt that these features result from the wisdom and lucidity of the Qur'an. The author modestly intends to serve as a means in humanity's search for Allah's right path. No material gain is sought in the publication of these works.

Considering these facts, those who encourage people to read these books, which open the "eyes" of the heart and guide them to become more devoted servants of Allah, render an invaluable service.

Meanwhile, it would just be a waste of time and energy to propagate other books which create confusion in peoples' minds, lead man into ideological chaos, and which, clearly have no strong and precise effects in removing the doubts in peoples' hearts, as also verified from previous experience. It is apparent that it is impossible for books devised to emphasize the author's literary power rather than the noble goal of saving people from loss of faith, to have such a great effect. Those who doubt this can readily see that the sole aim of Harun Yahya's books is to overcome disbelief and to disseminate the moral values of the Qur'an. The success and impact of this service are manifest in readers' conviction.

One point should be kept in mind: The main reason for the continuing cruelty, conflict, and all the ordeals the majority of people undergo is the ideological prevalence of disbelief. This state can only be ended with the ideological defeat of disbelief and by conveying the wonders of creation and Qur'anic morality so that people can live by it. Considering the state of the world today, which leads people into the downward spiral of violence, corruption and conflict, it is clear that this service has to be provided more speedily and effectively. Otherwise, it may be too late.

It is no exaggeration to say that the collection of books by Harun Yahya have assumed this leading role. By the will of Allah, these books will be a means through which people in the 21st century will attain the peace, justice and happiness promised in the Qur'an.

First published by Ta-Ha Publishers Ltd.

For information address:

Ta-Ha Publishers Ltd.

1 Wynne Road London SW9 OBB

Website: http://www.taha.co.uk

E-Mail: sales@taha.co.uk

ISBN 1 89794087 4

Printing Press: Secil Ofset
100 Yıl Mahallesi MAS-SIT Matbaacilar Sitesi
4. Cadde No:77 Bagcilar - Istanbul / TURKEY
Tel: (+90) 212 629 06 15

Printed and bound by:

Araştırma Publishing, 2002

Prof. Kazim Ismail Gurkan Cad.

Hamam Sokak Yavuz Han No.2/ K.6

Cagaloglu-Istanbul / Turkey

Tel.: (+90 212) 511 72 30

Website: www.harunyahya.com

E-Mail: info@harunyahya.com

CONTENTS

Preface

These are some of the stories of communities which We relate unto thee: of them some are standing, and some have been mown down (by the sickle of time). It was not We that wronged them: They wronged Their own souls: the deities, other than Allah, whom they invoked, profited them no whit when there issued the decree of thy Lord: Nor did they add aught (to their lot) but perdition! (Surah Hud: 100-101)

Allah creates man, and gives him a spiritual and physical form, lets him lead a certain course of life, and then will take him into His presence by bringing about his death. Allah creates man and according to the verse "Should He not know - He that created?" (Surat al-Mulk: 14), He is the One Who knows and recognises him, who educates him and meets his needs. Therefore, the only real purpose man has in life is to praise Allah, supplicate Him and worship Him. For the same reason, the pure message, and the revelation of Allah communicated to people through His messengers is the sole guidance for man.

The Qur'an is the last book of Allah and His only unaltered revelation.

This is why we are responsible for assuming the Qur'an as our true guide, and of being extremely meticulous about all its judgements. This is the only way for salvation both here in this world and beyond.

Therefore, we need to explore very carefully and attentively what the Qur'an relates to us and contemplate it. In the Qur'an, Allah states that the purpose of the Qur'an's revelation is to lead people to think:

Here is a Message for mankind: Let them take warning therefrom, and let them know that He is (no other than) One Allah: let men of understanding take heed. (Surah Ibrahim: 52)

The news of previous peoples which constitutes a great part of the Qur'an, is certainly one of the matters we ought to contemplate. A majority of these people rejected the prophets sent to them and, moreover, showed animosity towards them. Because of their audacity, they brought Allah's wrath upon themselves and have been wiped off the face of the earth.

The Qur'an tells us that these cases of destruction should be a warning for succeeding generations. For instance, right after the description of the punishment given to a group of Jews who rebelled against Allah, it is said in the Qur'an; "So We made it an example to their own time and to their posterity, and a lesson to those who fear Allah."(Surat al-Baqara: 66)

In this book, we will review some past societies that have been destroyed because of their rebellion against Allah. Our purpose is to highlight all these incidents, each of which is an "example to their own time", so that they can set a "warning".

The second reason we are examining these destructions is to show the manifestations of the verses of the Qur'an externally in the world and show the authenticity of the Qur'an's account. In the Qur'an, Allah certifies that His verses are observable in the external world: "Praise be to Allah, Who will soon show you His Signs, so that ye shall know them" (Surat an-Naml: 93)

And to know and identify them is one of the primary ways leading to faith

Nearly all the incidents of destruction related in the Qur'an have become "observable" and "identifiable" thanks to the current archive studies and archaeological finds. In this study, we will deal with the traces of some of the cases of destruction mentioned in the Qur'an. (It should be noted that some of the communities related in the Qur'an have not been included in the scope of this book, because in the Qur'an no specific time and place is given for some of them, which are only described for their rebellious conduct and antagonism towards Allah and His prophets, and for the disasters that befell them as a result. Thus, people are summoned to derive a warning from them)

Our purpose is to cast a light upon the realities of the Qur'an through contemporary discoveries and thus show the truth of Allah's religion to everyone- both believers and unbelievers.

Introduction:

Past Generations

Hath not the story reached them of those before them?- the People of Nuh, and 'Ad, and Thamud; the People of Ibrahim, the men of Madyan, and the cities overthrown. To them came their messengers with clear signs. It is not Allah Who wrongs them, but they wrong their own souls.
(Surat at-Tawba: 70)

The divine message, conveyed to the people by Allah through His messengers, has been communicated to us since the creation of man. Some societies have accepted the message while others have denied it. Occasionally, a minority from a society which accepted the message followed a messenger.

But the majority of communities who have received the message have not accepted it. They not only disregarded the message proclaimed by the messenger, but also tried to do harm to the messenger and his followers. The messengers were generally accused slanderously of "falsehood, magic, insanity and conceit" and leaders of many peoples even sought to have them murdered.

All that the prophets wanted from their people was their obedience to Allah. They did not ask for money or any other worldly gain in return. Nor did they try compel their people. What they did was only to invite their people to the religion of truth and that they should start a different way of life together with their followers apart from that community.

What has happened between Shu'ayb and the Madyan people to whom he was sent, illustrates the aforementioned prophet-community relationship. The reaction of Shu'ayb's tribe to Shu'ayb, who called them to believe in Allah and give up the injustices they had been doing, and the way they ended up are very interesting:

To the Madyan People (We sent) Shu'ayb, one of their own brethren: he said: "O my people! worship Allah: Ye have no other god but Him. And give not short measure or weight: I see you in prosperity, but I fear for you the penalty of a day that will compass (you) all round.

And O my people! give just measure and weight, nor withhold from the people the things that are their due: commit not evil in the land with intent to do mischief.

That which is left you by Allah is best for you, if ye (but) believed! but I am not set over you to keep watch!"

They said: "O Shu'ayb! Does thy (religion of) prayer command thee that we leave off the worship which our fathers practiced, or that we leave off doing what we like with our property? truly, thou art the one that forbeareth with faults and is right-minded!"

He said: "O my people! see ye whether I have a Clear (Sign) from my Lord, and He hath given me sustenance (pure and) good as from Himself? I wish not, in opposition to you, to do that which I forbid you to do. I only desire (your) betterment to the best of my power; and my success (in my task) can only come from Allah. In Him I trust, and unto Him I look.

And O my people! let not my dissent (from you) cause you to sin, lest ye suffer a fate similar to that of the people of Nuh or of Hud or of Salih, nor are the people of Lut far off from you! But ask forgiveness of your Lord, and turn unto Him (in repentance): For my Lord is indeed full of mercy and loving-kindness."

They said: "O Shu'ayb! much of what thou sayest we do not understand! In fact among us we see that thou hast no strength! Were it not for thy family, we should certainly have stoned thee! for thou hast among us no great position!"

He said: "O my people! is then my family of more consideration with you than Allah? For ye cast Him away behind your backs (with contempt). But verily my Lord encompasseth on all sides all that ye do! And O my people! Do whatever ye can: I will do (my part): Soon will ye know who it is on whom descends the penalty of ignominy; and who is a liar! and watch ye! for I too am watching with you!"

When Our decree issued, We saved Shu'ayb and those who believed with him, by (special) mercy from Ourselves: But the (mighty) blast did seize the wrong-doers, and they lay prostrate in their homes by the morning,- As if they had never dwelt and flourished there! Ah! Behold! How the Madyan were removed (from sight) as were removed the Thamud! (Surah Hud: 84-95)

Devising to "stone Shu'ayb", who had done nothing but summon them to goodness, the Madyan people were punished by the wrath of Allah and they perished as described in the verses above. The Madyan people are not the sole example. On the contrary, as Shu'ayb noted while talking with his people, many previous communities before the Madyan people had perished. After Madyan, many other communities also were destroyed by Allah's wrath.

In the following pages, we will describe the aforementioned communities which perished and their remnants. In the Qur'an, these communities are described in detail and people are invited to ponder on and take warning from how these people ended up.

At this point, the Qur'an particularly draws attention to the fact that the majority of the communities which perished had established high civilisations. In the Qur'an, this characteristic of the communities which perished is stressed as follows;

But how many generations before them did We destroy (for their sins) - stronger in power than they? Then did they wander through the land: was there any place of escape (for them)? (Surah Qaf: 36)

In the verse, two characteristics of the peoples which perished are particularly emphasised. The first is their being "stronger in power". This conveys that the communities which perished had established disciplined and strong military-bureaucratic systems and snatched power in the territory they lived through force. The second point is that the aforementioned communities founded big cities distinguished by their architectural characteristics.

It is noteworthy that both of these characteristics belong well to the current civilisation, which has established an elaborate world-culture through today's technology and science, and has founded centralised states, huge cities, yet denies and ignores Allah, forgetting that all is made possible by His power. But, as it is said in the verse, the civilisations they established could not save the communities which perished, since their civilisations were based on the denial of Allah. The end of today's civilisation will not be different as long as it is based on denial and mischief on earth.

A considerable number of the incidents of destruction, some of which are related in the Qur'an, have been confirmed by archaeological research made in modern times. These findings, which definitely prove that these incidents cited in the Qur'an have occurred, elucidate the need to be "forewarned" which features so much in the Qur'anic anecdotes. Allah tells us in the Qur'an that it is necessary to "travel through the earth" and "see what was the end of those before us".

> Nor did We send before thee (as messengers) any but men, whom we did inspire - (men) living in human habitations. Do they not travel through the earth, and see what was the end of those before them? But the home of the hereafter is best, for those who do right. Will ye not then understand?
> (Respite will be granted) until, when the messengers give up hope (of their people) and (come to) think that they were treated as liars, there reaches them Our help, and those whom We will are delivered into safety. But never will be warded off our punishment from those who are in sin.
> There is, in their stories, instruction for men endued with understanding. It is not a tale invented, but a confirmation of what went before it - a detailed exposition of all things, and a guide and a mercy to any such as believe. (Surah Yusuf: 109-111)

Indeed, there are examples in the stories of past communities for people endowed with understanding. Having perished because of their rebellion against Allah and their rejection of His commands, those communities reveal to us how weak and impotent mankind are with respect to Allah. In the following pages, we will examine these examples in a chronological order.

Chapter 1

Nuh's Flood

We (once) sent Nuh to his people,
and he tarried among them a thousand years less
fifty: but the Deluge overwhelmed them
while they (persisted in) sin.
(Surat al-Ankaboot: 14)

Referred to in nearly all cultures, Nuh's (Noah) Flood is one of the instances most widely alluded in the Qur'an. The indifference of the prophet Nuh's people to his advice and warnings, their reactions and how the event took place are told in detail in many verses.

The prophet Nuh was sent to warn his people who had turned away from Allah's verses and were associating partners with Him and to urge them to worship Allah only and abandon their rebellion. Despite the messenger Nuh advising his people many times to submit to Allah's commands and warning them of the wrath of Allah, they still denied him and continued associating partners with Allah. In Surat al-Mumenoon, how the affair developed is described as follows;

(Further, We sent a long line of prophets for your instruction). We sent Nuh to his people: He said, "O my people! worship Allah! Ye have no other god but Him. Will ye not fear (Him)?"
The chiefs of the Unbelievers among his people said: "He is no more than a man like yourselves: his wish is to assert his superiority over you: if Allah had wished (to send messengers), He could have sent down angels; never did we hear such a thing (as he says), among our ancestors of old."
(And some said): "He is only a man possessed: wait (and have patience) with him for a time."
(Nuh) said: "O my Lord! help me: for that they accuse me of falsehood!"
(Surat al-Mumenoon: 23-26)

As told in these verses, the chiefs of the community tried to accuse the prophet Nuh of trying to assert his superiority over them, that is, of seeking personal interests such as status, leadership and wealth, and they tried to identify him as "possessed", and they decided to bear with him for a while, and keep him under pressure.

Upon this, Allah told the messenger Nuh that those who rejected faith and did wrong would be punished by drowning and that those who believed would be saved.

Indeed when the time of punishment came, waters and overflowing springs burst from the ground and which, together with excessive rains, caused a huge flood. Allah told Nuh to "take on board pairs of every species, male and female, and his family- except those of them against whom the Word has already gone forth". All the people in that land were drowned in water - including Nuh's "son" who thought that he could be saved by taking refuge in a nearby mountain. All were drowned except those who embarked on the Ark with the prophet Nuh. When the waters abated at the end of the Flood, and "the matter was ended", the Ark came to rest on Judi - that is, on a high place - as the Qur'an informs us.

Archaeological, geological and historical studies show that this incident took place just as it is related in the Qur'an. The Flood is also very similarly described in many records of past civilisations and in many historical documents, although character and place-names vary, and "all that happened to an astray people" is presented to contemporary people as a warning.

Apart from the Old and New Testaments, the account of the Flood is told in a very similar manner in Sumerian and Assyrian-Babylonian records, in Greek legends, in the Shatapatha, Brahmana and Mahabharata epics of India, in some Welsh legends of the British Isles, in the Nordic Edda, in Lithuanian legends and even in some Chinese-rooted stories.

How could such detailed and pertinent information be gathered from such geographically and culturally distant lands, which are quite far from each other and from the flood region?

The answer is clear: the fact that the same incident is related in the records and inscriptions of all those communities which have little possibi-lity of communicating with each other, is in fact a clear evidence that these people received knowledge from a divine source. It seems that the Flood, one of the biggest and most destructive events in history, was narrated by many prophets sent to various civilisations for the purpose of setting an example. Thus news about the Flood has spread out to various cultures.

Besides, despite being narrated in many cultures and religious sources, the story of the Flood incident and of the prophet Nuh have been greatly altered and so have diverged from the original version because of falsification of sources, or incorrect transmission and maybe even wrong intentions. Research reveals that, among all the Flood narrations which relate basically the same event with various differences, the only consistent description is the one in the Qur'an.

The Prophet Nuh and the Flood in the Qur'an

Nuh's Flood is mentioned in many verses of the Qur'an. Below are found the verse arranged according to the sequence of events;

The Prophet Nuh's Inviting His People to the Religion of truth

We sent Nuh to his people. He said: "O my people! worship Allah! ye have no other god but Him. I fear for you the punishment of a dreadful day!" (Surat al-Araf: 59)

(Nuh:) "I am to you a messenger worthy of all trust: So fear Allah, and obey me. No reward do I ask of you for it: my reward is only from the Lord of the Worlds: So fear Allah, and obey me." (Surat ash-Shuara: 107-110)

(Further, We sent a long line of prophets for your instruction). We sent Nuh to his people: He said, "O my people! worship Allah! Ye have no other god but Him. Will ye not fear (Him)?" (Surat al-Mumenoon: 23)

The Prophet Nuh's Warning His People Against the Punishment of Allah

We sent Nuh to his People (with the Command): "Do thou warn thy People before there comes to them a grievous Penalty." (Surah Nuh: 1)

(Nuh:) "But soon will ye know who it is on whom will descend a penalty that will cover them with shame - on whom will be unloosed a penalty lasting" (Surah Hud: 39)

(Nuh:) "That ye serve none but Allah: Verily I do fear for you the penalty of a grievous day." (Surah Hud: 26)

Denial of Nuh's People

The leaders of his people said: "Ah! we see thee evidently wandering (in mind)." (Surat al-Araf: 60)

They said: "O Nuh! thou hast disputed with us, and (much) hast thou prolonged the dispute with us: now bring upon us what thou threatenest us with, if thou speakest the truth!?" (Surah Hud: 32)

Forthwith he (starts) constructing the Ark: Every time that the chiefs of his people passed by him, they threw ridicule on him. He said: "If ye ridicule us now, we (in our turn) can look down on you with ridicule likewise!" (Surah Hud: 38)

The chiefs of the Unbelievers among his people said: "He is no more than a man like yourselves: his wish is to assert his superiority over you: if Allah had wished (to send messengers), He could have sent down angels; never did we hear such a thing (as he says), among our ancestors of old." (And some said): "He is only a man possessed: wait (and have patience) with him for a time." (Surat al-Mumenoon: 24-25)

Before them the People of Nuh rejected (their messenger): they rejected Our servant, and said, "Here is one possessed!", and he was driven out. (Surat al-Qamar: 9)

Their Disregard of Those Who Followed the Prophet Nuh

But the chiefs of the Unbelievers among his people said: "We see (in) thee nothing but a man like ourselves: Nor do we see that any follow thee but the meanest among us, in judgment immature: Nor do we see in you (all) any merit above us: in fact we think ye are liars!" (Surah Hud: 27)

They said: "Shall we believe in thee when it is the meanest that follow thee?" He said: "And what do I know as to what they do? Their account is only with my Lord, if ye could (but) understand. I am not one to drive away those who believe. I am sent only to warn plainly in public." (Surat ash-Shuara: 111-115)

Allah's Reminding Nuh Not to Grieve

It was revealed to Nuh: "None of thy people will believe except those who have believed already! So grieve no longer over their (evil) deeds." (Surah Hud, 36)

Prayers of the prophet Nuh

(Nuh:) "Judge Thou, then, between me and them openly, and deliver me and those of the Believers who are with me." (Surat ash-Shuara: 118)

Then he called on his Lord: "I am one overcome: do Thou then help (me)!" (Surat al-Qamar: 10)

(Nuh:) He said: "O my Lord! I have called to my People night and day: But my call only increases (their) flight (from the Right)." (Surah Nuh: 5-6)

(Nuh) said: "O my Lord! help me: for that they accuse me of falsehood!" (Surat al-Mumenoon: 26)

(In the days of old), Nuh cried to Us, and We are the best to hear prayer. (Surat as-Saaffat: 75)

The Construction of the Ark

But construct an Ark under Our eyes and Our inspiration, and address Me no (further) on behalf of those who are in sin: for they are about to be overwhelmed (in the Flood). (Surah Hud: 37)

The Destruction of the prophet Nuh's People by Drowning

But they rejected him, and We delivered him, and those with him, in the Ark: but We overwhelmed in the flood those who rejected Our signs. They were indeed a blind people! (Surat al-Araf: 64)

Thereafter We drowned those who remained behind. (Surat ash-Shuara: 120)

We (once) sent Nuh to his people, and he tarried among them a thousand years less fifty: but the Deluge overwhelmed them while they (persisted in) sin. (Surat al-Ankaboot: 14)

But they denied him so We rescued him, and all those with him, in the Ark and We made them the successors and We drowned the people who denied Our Signs. See the final fate of those who were warned! (Surah Yunus: 73)

The Destruction of the Prophet Nuh's "Son"

The Qur'an relates a dialogue between Nuh and his son, in the early stages of the Flood;

So the Ark floated with them on the waves (towering) like mountains, and Nuh called out to his son, who had separated himself (from the rest): "O my son! embark with us, and be not with the unbelievers!" The son replied: "I will betake myself to some mountain: it will save me from the water." Nuh said: "This day nothing can save, from the command of Allah, any but those on whom He hath mercy!" And the waves came between them, and the son was among those overwhelmed in the Flood. (Surah Hud: 42-43)

Saving the Believers from the Flood

So We delivered him and those with him, in the Ark filled (with all creatures). (Surat ash-Shuara: 119)
But We saved him and the companions of the Ark, and We made the (Ark) a Sign for all peoples! (Surat al-Ankaboot: 15)

The Physical Nature of the Flood

So We opened the gates of heaven, with water pouring forth. And We caused the earth to gush forth with springs, so the waters met (and rose) to the extent decreed. But We bore him on an (Ark) made of broad planks and caulked with palm-fibre: (Surat al-Qamar: 11-13)
At length, behold! there came Our command, and the fountains of the earth gushed forth! We said: "Embark therein, of each kind two, male and female, and your family - except those against whom the word has already gone forth - and the Believers." but only a few believed with him.
So the Ark floated with them on the waves (towering) like mountains, and Nuh called out to his son, who had separated himself (from the rest): "O my son! embark with us, and be not with the unbelievers!"(Surah Hud: 40-42)
So We inspired him (with this message): "Construct the Ark within Our sight and under Our guidance: then when comes Our Command, and the fountains of the earth gush forth, take thou on board pairs of every species, male and female, and thy family- except those of them against whom the Word has already gone forth: And address Me not in favour of the wrong-doers;

for they shall be drowned (in the Flood)." (Surat al-Mumenoon: 27)

The Resting of the Ark on a High Place

Then the word went forth: "O earth! swallow up thy water, and O sky! Withhold (thy rain)!" and the water abated, and the matter was ended. The Ark rested on Mount Judi, and the word went forth: "Away with those who do wrong!" (Surah Hud: 44)

The Instructional Aspect of the Flood Incident

We, when the water (of Nuh's Flood) overflowed beyond its limits, carried you (mankind), in the floating (Ark), That We might make it a Message unto you, and that ears (that should hear the tale and) retain its memory should bear its (lessons) in remembrance. (Surat al-Haaqqa: 11-12)

Allah's Praise of the Prophet Nuh

Peace and salutation to Nuh among the nations! Thus indeed do we reward those who do right. For he was one of our believing Servants. (Surat as-Saaffat: 79-81)

Was the Flood a Local Disaster or was It Global?

Those who deny the reality of Nuh's Flood, support their stance with the assertion that a worldwide flood is impossible. However, their denial of any flood whatsoever is also directed as an attack on the Qur'an. According to them, all the revealed books including the Qur'an, appear to defend the reality of a worldwide flood and are thus mistaken.

Yet this denial of the Qur'an is not true. The Qur'an was revealed by Allah and is the sole unaltered divine book. The Qur'an looks at the Flood from a very different viewpoint than do the Pentateuch and the other flood legends narrated in various cultures. The Pentateuch, a name for the first five books of the Old Testament, says that the flood was global; that it covered the whole world. Yet the Qur'an does not offer such as assertion, indeed on the contrary, the relevant verses imply that the Flood was regional and did not cover the whole world but only drowned Nuh's people who had been warned by Nuh and so were punished.

When the Flood narrations of the Old Testament and the Qur'an are examined, this difference is plain. The Old Testament, which has been subject to so many alterations and additions throughout its history that it can truly be said that almost nothing of the original remains, describes how the Flood began as follows;

> And God saw that the wickedness of man was great in the earth, and that every imagination of the thoughts of his heart was only evil continually. And it repented the LORD that he had made man on the earth, and it grieved him at his heart. And the LORD said, I will destroy man whom I have created from the face of the earth; both man, and beast, and the creeping thing, and the fowls of the air; for it repenteth me that I have made them. But Noah found grace in the eyes of the LORD (Genesis, 6:5-8)

However, in the Qur'an, it is clearly shown that it was not the whole world, but only Nuh's people who were destroyed. Just as Hud was sent only to 'Ad (Surah Hud: 50), Salih was sent to Thamud (Surah Hud: 61) and all the other prophet prior to Muhammad were sent only to their own peoples, Nuh was sent only to his people and the flood caused only Nuh's people to disappear;

> We sent Nuh to his people (with a mission): "I have come to you with a Clear Warning: That ye serve none but Allah: Verily I do fear for you the penalty of a grievous day." (Surah Hud: 25-26)

Those who perished were people who totally disregarded Prophet Nuh's proclamation of the message and persisted on rebellion. Relevant verses are explicit enough to leave no room for discussion:

> But they rejected him, and We delivered him, and those with him, in the Ark: but We overwhelmed in the flood those who rejected Our signs. They were indeed a blind people! (Surat al-Araf: 64)

> But they denied him so We rescued him, and all those with him, in the Ark and We made them the successors and We drowned the people who denied Our Signs. See the final fate of those who were warned! (Surah Yunus: 73)

Besides, in the Qur'an, Allah remarks that He does not destroy a community unless a messenger has been sent to it. Destruction can only take place if a warner has already arrived among a particular people and the warner is belied. Allah states in Surat al-Qasas;

> Nor was thy Lord the one to destroy a population until He had sent to its centre a messenger, rehearsing to them Our Signs; nor are We going to destroy a population except when its members practice iniquity. (Surat al-Qasas: 59)

It is not Allah's way to destroy people whom He has not sent any messengers. As a warner, Nuh had been sent only to his people. Therefore, Allah did not destroy the communities who had not been sent a warner, but only Nuh's people.

From these statements in the Qur'an, we can be certain that Nuh's flood was a regional disaster, not a global one. The excavations made in the archaeological region where the flood is supposed to have happened - which we will examine here below - show that the flood was not a global event affecting the whole world, but a very broad catastrophe which affected a certain part of Mesopotamia.

Were all the Animals Taken on Board?

The interpreters of the Bible believe that Nuh took all animal species on earth on board the Ark and that animals were saved from extinction thanks to Nuh. According to this belief, a pair of every land dwelling species on earth were brought together and put on board.

Those who defend this assertion doubtless have to face serious difficulties in many respects. The question of how the animal species taken aboard were fed, how they were housed on the Ark, or how they were isolated from each other are impossible to answer. Moreover, the question remains: how were animals from different continents brought together - mammals in the poles, kangaroos in Australia or the bison peculiar to America? Moreover, there follow more questions as to how very dangerous animals - venomous ones like snakes, scorpions and wild animals - were caught and how they could be sustained away from their natural habitats until the flood abated.

These are the questions which the Old Testament faces. In the Qur'an, there is no statement implying that all the animal species on earth were taken on board. As we have noted before, the Flood took place in a certain region. Therefore, the animals taken on board could only have been those living in the region where Nuh's people resided.

However, it is evident that it is impossible even to collect all the animal species living in that region. It is difficult to think of Nuh and a few number of believers beside him (Surah Hud: 40) going in all directions and setting out to collect two each of hundreds of animal species in their surroundings. It is even more highly improbable for them to have collected specimens of the insect species living in their region, and, moreover, to discriminate the males from the female! This is the reason why it is more probable that the animals collected were those that could easily be caught and sustained, and were, therefore, domestic animals especially useful to man. The prophet Nuh was most likely to have taken on board such animals as cows, sheep, horses, poultry camels and the like, because these were the primary animals that would have been needed for establishing a new life in a region which would have lost a great deal of its livestock because of the Flood.

Here the important point is that the divine wisdom in Allah's command to Nuh to collect the animals lies in its being directed to the collecting of the animals required for the new life to be established after the flood rather than to protecting the genus of animals. Since the flood was regional, the extinction of animal species could not have been a possibility. It is most likely that after the flood, animals from other regions would have migrated to that area in the course of time, and re-populated the region with its old liveliness. What was important was the life to be established in the region right after the flood, and the animals gathered would have been collected basically for this purpose.

How High Did the Waters Arise?

Another debate around the Flood is whether the waters rose high enough to cover the mountains. As acknowledged, the Qur'an informs us that the Ark came to rest on "al-Judi" after the flood. The word "Judi" is generally referred to as a specific mountain site, whereas the word appears to mean "high setting or hill" in Arabic. Therefore it should not be forgotten that in the Qur'an, "Judi" could have been used not as a name for a specific mountain site but to indicate that the Ark had come to rest on a high site. Besides, the aforementioned meaning of the word "Judi" may also show that the waters had reached to a certain height, but not as high as mountaintop level. That is to say that the flood most probably did not engulf the whole earth and all the mountains as described in the Old Testament, but only covered a certain region.

The Location of Nuh's Flood

The Mesopotamian Plains have been suggested as the location of the Flood. In this region were the oldest civilisations known to history. Besides, being between the Tigris and Euphrates rivers, this region geographically is a suitable setting for a great deluge. One of the contributory factors to the effect of the flood is most probably that these two rivers overflowed their beds and overwhelmed the region.

The second reason why this region is regarded as the location for the Flood is historical. In the records of many civilisations of the region many documents are to be found referring to a flood that took place in the same period. Having witnessed the destruction of Nuh's people, these civilisations must have felt the need to record how this disaster came about and in what it resulted. It is known that most of the legends on the flood are of Mesopotamian origin. More important to us are the archaeological finds. These show that a big deluge did indeed once befall this region. As we will examine in detail in the following pages, this flood caused civilisation to be suspended for a period. In the excavations, apparent traces of such an enormous disaster have been unearthed.

The excavations made in the Mesopotamian region disclose that many times in history, this region suffered from various disasters as a result of deluges and the overflow of the Tigris and Euphrates rivers. For instance around 2nd millennium BC, at the time of Ibbi-sin, ruler of the large nation of Ur situated to the south of Mesopotamia, a year is marked as "coming after a Flood that annihilated the borders between the heavens and the earth"[1] . Around 1700 BC, at the time of the Babylonian Hammurabi, a year is marked as being that in which occurred the incident of "the ruining of the city of Eshnunna with a deluge".

In the 10th Century BC, at the time of the ruler Nabu-mukin-apal, a deluge occurred in the city of Babylon.[2] After 'Isa (Jesus), in the 7th, 8th, 10th, 11th, and 12th centuries, important deluges took place in the region. In the 20th Century, the same happened in 1925, 1930 and 1954.[3] It is clear that the region has always been subject to the disaster of flooding and, as indicated in the Qur'an, it is very likely that a massive flood could have destroyed an entire people.

An illustration depicting Nuh's Flood.

Archaeological Evidence of the Flood

It is no coincidence that today we run into traces of most of the communities which are said in the Qur'an to have been destroyed. Archaeological evidence yields the fact that the more suddenly a community disappears, the more likely it is that we will come across some of its remnants.

In the case of a civilisation suddenly disappearing, which can happen as a result of a natural disaster, sudden emigration or war, the traces of this civilisation can often be preserved much better. Houses in which people lived and tools they once used in daily life are buried under the earth in a short time. Thus these are preserved for quite long periods untouched by human hand and they yield important evidence of the past when brought into daylight.

This is how a great deal of evidence for Nuh's Flood has been uncovered in our day. Thought to have been occurred around the 3rd millennium BC., the Flood put an end to a whole civilisation in a moment, and later caused a brand new civilisation to be established in its stead. Thus the apparent evidence for the Flood has been preserved for thousands of years so that we may take warning.

Many excavations have been made in investigation of the flood which covered the Mesopotamian plains. In excavations made in the region, in four main cities there are found traces of what must have been a particularly large flood. These cities were the important cities of Mesopotamia: Ur, Erech, Kish and Shuruppak.

The excavations made in these cities reveal that all four of these were subjected to a flood around the 3rd millennium BC.

First let's take a look at the excavations made in the city of Ur.

The oldest remains of a civilisation unearthed in the excavations made in the city of Ur, which has been re-named "Tell al Muqqayar" in our day, date back as far as 7000 BC. As one of the sites which has been home to one of the earliest civilisations, the city of Ur has been a region of settlements in which many cultures succeeded each other.

Archaeological findings from the city of Ur show that here civilisation was interrupted after an enormous flood, and that then new civilisations later emerged. R.H. Hall from the British Museum made the first excavations here. Leonard Woolley, who took upon himself to carry on with excavations after Hall, also supervised an excavation organised collectively by the British Museum and the University of Pennsylvania. Excavations conducted by Woolley, which had a huge effect world-wide, lasted from 1922 to 1934.

Sir Woolley's excavations took place in the middle of the desert between Baghdad and the Persian Gulf. The first founders of the city of Ur were a people who had come from North Mesopotamia and called themselves "Ubaidian". Excavations originally began to gather information on these people. Woolley's excavations are described by the German archaeologist Werner Keller as follows;

"The graves of the kings of Ur" - so Woolley, in the exuberance of his delight at discovering them, had dubbed the tombs of Sumerian nobles whose truly regal splendour had been exposed when the spades of the archaeologists attacked a fifty-foot mound south of the temple and found a long row of superimposed graves. The stone vaults were veritable treasure chests, for they were filled with all the costly goblets, wonderfully shaped jugs and vases, bronze tableware, mother of pearl mosaics, lapis lazuli, and silver surrounded these bodies which had mouldered into dust. Harps and lyres rested against the walls. "Almost at once" he wrote later in his diary, "discoveries were made which confirmed our suspicions. Directly under the floor of one of the tombs of the kings we found in a layer of charred wood ash numerous clay tablets, which were covered with characters of a much older type than the inscriptions on the graves. Judging by the nature of the writing, the tablets could be assigned to about 3000 BC. They were therefore two or three centuries earlier than the tombs".

The shafts went deeper and deeper. New strata, with fragments of jars, pots, and bowls, kept appearing. The experts noticed that the pottery remained surprisingly enough unchanged. It looked exactly like that which had been found in the graves of the kings. Therefore, it seemed that for centuries the Sumerian civilisation had undergone no radical change. They must, according to the conclusion, have reached a high level of development astonishingly early.

When after several days some of Woolley's workmen called out to him, "We are on ground level", he let himself down onto the floor of the shaft to sa-

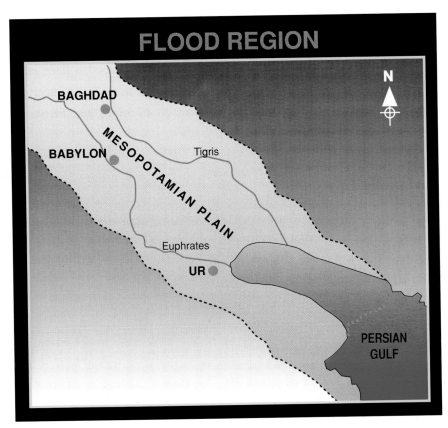

FLOOD REGION

BAGHDAD

BABYLON

MESOPOTAMIAN PLAIN

Tigris

Euphrates

UR

PERSIAN GULF

N

According to archaeological finds, Nuh's Flood took place on the Mesopotamian plains. The plains had a different shape then. In the above diagram, the current borders of the plains are denoted with a red cut line. The large section lying behind the red line is known to have been a part of the sea at that time.

tisfy himself. Woolley's first thought was "This is it at last". It was sand, pure sand of a kind that could only have been deposited by water.

They decided to dig on and make the shaft deeper. Deeper and deeper went the spades into the ground: three feet, six feet - still pure mud. Suddenly, at ten feet, the layer of mud stopped as abruptly as it had started. Under this clay deposit of almost ten feet thick, they had struck fresh evidence of human habitation. The appearance and quality of the pottery had noticeably altered. Here, they were handmade. Metal remains were nowhere to be found. The primitive implement that did emerge was made of hewn flint. It must belong to the Stone Age!

The Flood - that was the only possible explanation of this great clay deposit beneath the hill at Ur, which quite clearly separated two epochs of settlement. The sea had left its unmistakable traces in the shape of remains of little marine organisms embedded in the mud. [4]

Microscopic analysis revealed that this great clay deposit beneath the hill at Ur had accumulated here as a result of a flood so big as to annihilate ancient Sumerian civilisation. The epic of Gilgamesh and the story of Nuh were united in this shaft dug deep under the Mesopotamian desert.

Max Mallowan related the thoughts of Leonard Woolley, who said that such a huge mass of alluvium formed in a single time slice could only be the result of a huge flood disaster. Woolley also described the flood layer that separated the Sumerian city of Ur from the city of Al-Ubaid whose inhabitants used painted pottery, as the remains of the Flood.[5]

These show that the city of Ur was one of the places affected by the Flood. Werner Keller expressed the importance of the aforementioned excavation by saying that the yield of city-remains beneath a muddy layer in

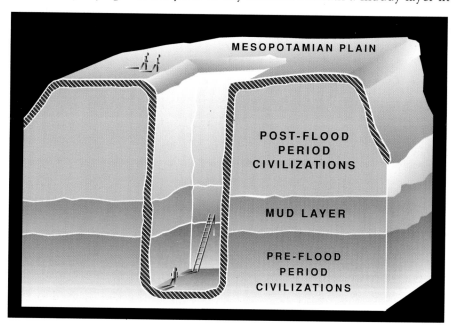

The excavations made by Sir Leonard Woolley in the Mesopotamian plains disclosed the presence of a mud-clay layer 2.5 m. deep in the earth. This mud-clay layer was most probably formed by the clay masses carried by the flood waters and, in the whole world, it only exists under the Mesopotamian plains. This discovery became an important piece of evidence proving that the Flood had only occurred on the Mesopotamian plains.

the archaeological excavations made in Mesopotamia proves that there was a flood here.[6]

Another Mesopotamian city carrying traces of the Flood is "Kish of the Sumerians" which is now known as Tall Al-Uhaimer. According to ancient Sumerian sources, this city was the "seat of the first postdiluvian dynasty"[7]

The city of Shuruppak in South Mesopotamia, which is today named as Tall Fa'rah, likewise carries apparent traces of the Flood. Archaeological studies in this city were headed by Erich Schmidt from the University of Pennsylvania between 1920-1930. These excavations uncovered three layers of habitation extending in time from the late prehistoric period to the 3rd dynasty of Ur (2112-2004 BC). The most distinctive finds were ruins of well-built houses along with cuneiform tablets of administrative records and lists of words, indicating a highly developed society already in being toward the end of the 4th millennium BC. [8]

The main point is that a big flood disaster was understood to have occurred in this city around 2900-3000 BC. According to Mallowan's account, 4-5 metres below the earth, Schmidt had reached a yellow soil layer (formed by flood) made up of a mixture of clay and sand. This layer was closer to the plain level than the tumulus profile and it could be observed all around the tumulus... Schmidt defined this layer made up of a mixture of clay and sand, which remained from the time of Ancient Kingdom of Cemdet Nasr, as "a sand with its origins in the river" and associated it with Nuh's Flood.[9]

In the excavations made in the city of Shuruppak, the remains of a flood were found that corresponded approximately to the years 2900-3000 BC. Probably, the city of Shuruppak was probably as much effected by the flood as the other cities.[10]

The latest place which is shown to have been affected by the Flood is the city of Erech to the south of Shuruppak which is known as Tall Al-Warka today. In this city just as in others, a flood layer is found. This flood layer is dated between 2900-3000 BC just like the others. [11]

As is well known, the Tigris and Euphrates rivers cut across Mesopotamia from one end to the other. It seems that, during the event, these two rivers and many other water resources, big and small, overflowed and, by uniting with rain water, caused a big deluge. The event is described in the Qur'an;

> So We opened the gates of heaven, with water pouring forth. And We caused the earth to gush forth with springs, so the waters met (and rose) to the extent decreed. (Surat al-Qamar: 11-12)

When the factors causing the Flood are examined one by one, it is seen that they all appear as very natural phenomena. What makes the event miraculous is their taking place at the same time and Nuh's warning his people about such a disaster beforehand.

Assessment of the evidence obtained from the completed studies revealed that the Flood area stretches approximately 160 km. (in width) from east to west, and 600 km. (in length) from north to south. This shows that the Flood covered all the Mesopotamian plains. When we examine the order of the cities Ur, Erech, Shuruppak and Kish which bear the traces of the Flood, we see that these are lined along a route. Therefore, the Flood must have affected these four cities and their surroundings. Besides it should be noted that around 3000 BC, the geographical structure of the Mesopotamian plain was different from what it is now. At those times, the bed of the Euphrates river was more to the east than it is today; this stream-line was matched with a line passing through Ur, Erech, Shuruppak and Kish. With the opening of the "springs of the earth and heaven", it seems that the river Euphrates overflowed and spread thus destroying the four cities cited above.

Religions and Cultures Mentioning the Flood

The Flood has been made known to nearly all peoples through the mouth of prophets conveying the Religion of Truth, but it has been turned into legends by those communities and been both extended and corrupted on the way.

Allah has conveyed news of Nuh's Flood to people through messengers and books He has sent to different communities so that it may be a warning and example. Yet, each time the texts have been altered from their originals, and the Flood descriptions have been expanded with mythological elements. The Qur'an is the only remaining source that is in substantial agreement with the findings of empirical observation. This is only because Allah has guarded the Qur'an from undergoing even a single change and has not permitted it to be corrupted. According to the following judgment of the Qur'an "We have, without doubt, sent down the Message; and We will assuredly guard it (from corruption)" (Surat al-Hijr: 9) the Qur'an is under the special protection of Allah.

In the latest part of this chapter dealing with the Flood, we will see how the incident is envisioned - though quite corrupted - in various cultures and in the Old and New Testaments.

Nuh's Flood in the Old Testament

The book in truth revealed to the prophet Musa was the Tawrah. Almost nothing at all of this revelation remains, and the biblical book, the "Pentateuch", has long lost its connection to the original revelation over time. Even then most parts of that dubious entity have been altered by the rabbis of the Jewish community. Similarly, the revelations all the other prophets were sent with to the Children of Israel after the prophet Musa were subject to the same behaviour and greatly altered. Therefore, this characteristic, which calls us to rename it the "Altered Pentateuch" because it has lost its connection to its original, drives us to regard it as a product of human beings attempting to record their tribes' history rather than a divine book. Unsurprisingly, the nature of the Altered Pentateuch and the contradictions it contains are well revealed in its telling of the story of Nuh despite it having some parallelisms with the Qur'an in parts.

According to the Old Testament, God proclaimed Nuh that everybody except the believers would be destroyed because the earth was full of violence. To this end, He commanded him to make the Ark and described him in detail how to do it. He also told him to take along his family, his three sons, his sons' wives, two of every living thing and some provisions.

Seven days later, when the time for the Flood came, all the underground sources burst open, the window of the heavens opened and a big flood engulfed everything. This lasted for forty days and nights. The ship sailed over waters covering all mountains and high hills. Thus those who were on board with Nuh were saved and the rest were carried away by the waters of the Flood and were drowned to death. The rain stopped after the Flood, which lasted for 40 days and 40 nights, and the waters started to recede 150 days after that.

Thereafter, on the seventeenth day of the seventh month, the ship came to rest on the Ararat (Agri) mountains. Nuh sent out a dove to see whether the waters had fully receded or not and when finally the dove did not come back, he understood that the waters had totally receded. God told them to disembark from the ship and spread out on the earth.

One of the contradictions in this story in the Old Testament is that, following this summary, in the "Yahwist" version of the text, it is said that God commanded Nuh to take along seven of those animals, males and females, He called "clean" and only pairs of those animals He called "unclean". This contradicts with the text above. Besides, in the Old Testament, the duration of the Flood is also different. According to the Yahwist account the rising of the waters took 40 days whereas it is said to be 150 days according to the account of the laymen.

Some parts of the Old Testament account of Nuh's Flood are as follows; And God said unto Noah, The end of all flesh is come before me; for the earth is filled with violence through them; and, behold, I will destroy them with the earth. Make thee an ark of gopher wood;...

...And, behold, I, even I, do bring a flood of waters upon the earth, to destroy all flesh, wherein [is] the breath of life, from under heaven; [and] every thing that [is] in the earth shall die. But with thee will I establish my covenant; and thou shalt come into the ark, thou, and thy sons, and thy wife, and thy sons' wives with thee. And of every living thing of all flesh, two of every [sort] shalt thou bring into the ark, to keep [them] alive with thee; they shall be male and female...

...Thus did Noah; according to all that God commanded him, so did he. (Genesis, 6: 13-22)

And the ark rested in the seventh month, on the seventeenth day of the month, upon the mountains of Ararat. (Genesis, 8: 4)

Of every clean beast thou shalt take to thee by sevens, the male and his female: and of beasts that [are] not clean by two, the male and his female. Of fowls also of the air by sevens, the male and the female; to keep seed alive upon the face of all the earth. (Genesis, 7:2-3)

And I will establish my covenant with you; neither shall all flesh be cut off any more by the waters of a flood; neither shall there any more be a flood to destroy the earth. (Genesis, 9:11)

According to the Old Testament, in accordance with the verdict that "every thing that [is] in the earth shall die" in a flood covering all the world, all people were punished, and the only ones who survived were those who embarked on the Ark with Nuh.

Nuh's Flood in the New Testament

The New Testament we have today is not a Divine book in the real sense of the word either. Being comprised of the words and deeds of 'Isa (Jesus), the New Testament starts with four "Gospels" written up to one century after 'Isa by people who had never seen him or kept company with him; namely, Matthew, Mark, Luke and John. There are very obvious contradictions between these four Gospels. Particularly, the Gospel of John differs to a great extent from the other three (Synoptic Gospels) which are to some degree, but not totally, compatible with each other. The other books of the New Testament comprise the letters written by the Apostles and Saul of Tarsus (later called Saint Paul) describing the deeds of the apostles after 'Isa.

Therefore the New Testament of today is not a Divine text, but rather a semi-historical book.

In the New Testament, Nuh's Flood is briefly described as follows; Nuh was sent as a messenger to a disobedient community who were astray, but his people did not follow him and went on in their perverseness. Upon this, Allah called those who rejected faith to account with the Flood and saved Nuh and the believers by putting them on the Ark. Some chapters of the New Testament related to the subject are as follows;

But as the days of Noe [were], so shall also the coming of the Son of man be. For as in the days that were before the flood they were eating and drinking, marrying and giving in marriage, until the day that Noe entered into the ark, And knew not until the flood came, and took them all away; so shall also the coming of the Son of man be. (Matthew, 24: 37-39)

And spared not the old world, but saved Noah the eighth [person], a preacher of righteousness, bringing in the flood upon the world of the ungodly. (Second Peter, 2: 5)

And as it was in the days of Noe, so shall it be also in the days of the Son of man. They did eat, they drank, they married wives, they were given in marriage, until the day that Noe entered into the ark, and the flood came, and destroyed them all. (Luke, 17: 26-27)

Which sometime were disobedient, when once the longsuffering of God waited in the days of Noah, while the ark was a preparing, wherein few, that is, eight souls were saved by water. (First Peter, 3: 20)

For this they willingly are ignorant of, that by the word of God the heavens were of old, and the earth standing out of the water and in the water: Whereby the world that then was, being overflowed with water, perished. (Second Peter, 3: 5-6)

Accounts of the Flood in Other Cultures

Sumer: A god called Enlil told people that other gods intended to destroy humanity, but that he himself was willing to save them. The hero of the story is Ziusudra, the devotee king of the city of Sippur. God Enlil told Ziusudra what to do to be saved from the Flood. The text relating the making of the boat is missing, but the fact that such a part once existed is revealed in the parts in which it is told how Ziusudra is saved. Relying on the Babylonian version of the flood, one reaches the conclusion that in the complete Sumerian version of the event there must have been much more comprehensive details of the reason for the Flood and how the boat was made.

Babylonia: Ut-Napishtim is the Babylonian counterpart of the Sumerian hero of the Flood, Ziusudra. Another important character is Gilgamesh. According to the legend, Gilgamesh decided to seek and find his ancestry to obtain the secret of immortality. He was warned against the dangers and difficulties of such a journey. He was told that he is supposed to make a journey in which he should pass over the "Mashu Mountains and waters of death"; and that such a journey had only been accomplished by the sun-god Shamash up until then. Still, Gilgamesh braved all the dangers of the journey and finally succeeded in reaching Ut-Napishtim.

The text is cut off at the point where the meeting of Gilgamesh and Ut-Napishtim is told; and when it next becomes legible, Ut-Napishtim said to Gilgamesh that "the gods reserved the secret of death and life to themselves" (that they did not give it to people). Upon this, Gilgamesh asked Ut-Napishtim how he had acquired immortality; and Ut-Napishtim told him the story of the flood as a reply to his question. The flood is also told in the famous "twelve tables" of the Gilgamesh epic.

Ut-Napishtim started by saying that the story he was about to tell Gilgamesh was "something secret, a secret of the gods". He said that he was from the city of Shuruppak, the oldest among the cities of the Akkad land. According to his account, the god "Ea" had called out to him through the walls of a cane hut and declared that the gods had decided to destroy all the seeds of life with a flood; but the reason of their decision was not explained in the Babylonian Flood account just as it had not been in the Sumerian Flood story. Ut-Napishtim said that Ea had told him to make a ship in which he should bring together and put the "seeds of all living things". He informed him of the size and shape of the ship; according to it, the width, length, and height of the ship were equal to each other. The storm turned everything upside down for six days and nights. On the seventh day it calmed down. Ut-Napishtim saw that on the outside, it had "turned into sticky mud". The ship came to rest on Mt. Nisir.

According to Sumerian and Babylonian records, Xisuthros or Khasisatra is saved from the Flood by a ship of 925 metres in length, along with his family, friends, and some birds and animals. It is said that "the waters outspread towards the heavens, the oceans covered the shores, and rivers overflowed from their beds". The ship then came to rest on the Corydaean mountain.

According to the Assyrian-Babylonian records, Ubar-Tutu or Khasisatra was saved along with his family, servants, flocks and wild animals on a ship which is 600 cubits long, 60 cubits high and wide. The Flood lasted for 6 days and 6 nights. When the ship reached the Nizar Mountain, the dove that was set free came back but the raven did not.

According to some Sumerian, Assyrian and Babylonian records, Ut-Na-pishtim with his family survived through the Flood which lasted for 6 days and 6 nights. It is said: "On the seventh day Ut-Napishtim looked outside. It was all very quite. Man had once more turned to mud.". When the ship came to rest on the Nizar mountain, Ut-Napishtim sent out one pigeon, one raven and one sparrow. The raven stayed to eat the corpses, but the other two birds did not return.

India: In the Shatapatha Brahmana and Mahabharata epics of India, the person called Manu is saved from the flood along with Rishiz. According to the legend, a fish which Manu caught and whose life he spared, suddenly grew and told him to make a ship and tie it to its horns. This fish was accepted to be a manifestation of the god Vishnu. The fish drove the ship over huge waves, and brought it to the north, the Hismavat mountain.

Wales: According to Welsh legend (from Wales, a Celtic region of Britain), Dwynwen and Dwyfach escaped from the great disaster on ship. When the dreadful deluge that occurred from the bursting of Llynllion, which was called the Lake of Waves, subsided, Dwywen and Dwyfach started to repopulate Britain afresh.

Scandinavia: Nordic Edda legends report that Bergalmir and his wife escaped from the flood in a big boat.

Lithuania: In Lithuanian legend, it is told that a few pairs of men and animals were saved by taking shelter in a crust up on the top of a lofty mountain. When the winds and floods that lasted for twelve days and twelve nights reached to the high mountain so much as almost to swallow those on it, the Creator threw a giant nut shell to them. Those on the mountain were saved from disaster by sailing in this nut shell.

China: Chinese sources relate that a person called Yao with seven other persons or Fa Li with his wife and children, were saved from the deluge and earthquakes on a sailing boat. It is said that "the earth was all in ruins. The waters burst forth and covered everywhere". Finally, the waters receded.

Nuh's Flood in Greek Mythology: The god Zeus decided to destroy people, who have become more wrongdoing every day, with a flood. Only Deucalion and his wife Pyrrha were saved from the flood, because Deucalion's father Prometheus had formerly advised his son to make a boat. The couple set foot on Mount Parnassos on the 9th day after embarking on the boat.

All these legends indicate a concrete historical reality. In history, each community received the message, everybody received Divine revelation, and thus many communities learned about the Flood. Unfortunately, as people turned away from the essence of the Divine revelation, the account of the Flood underwent many changes, and turned into legends and myths.

The only source where we can find the real story of Nuh and the people who denied him, is the Qur'an, which is the single unaltered source of Divine revelation remaining.

The Qur'an provides us with correct information not only on Nuh's Flood, but also about other historical events and peoples. In the following chapters, we will review these true stories.

Chapter 2

The Prophet Ibrahim's Life

Ibrahim was not a Jew nor yet a Christian;
but he was true in Faith,
and bowed his will to Allah's (Which is Islam),
and he joined not gods with Allah.
Without doubt, among men, the nearest of kin to Ibrahim, are
those who follow him, as are also this Prophet and those who believe: And
Allah is the Protector of those who have faith.
(Surah Aal-e Imran: 67-68)

The prophet Ibrahim (Abraham) is often referred to in the Qur'an and is distinguished by Allah as an example to people. He conveyed the message of Allah to his people who worshipped idols and he warned them so that they might fear Allah. His people did not listen to his warnings but, on the contrary, opposed him. When the oppression of his people increased, Ibrahim had to move elsewhere with his wife, the prophet Lut and possibly a few other people who went with them.

Ibrahim was descended from Nuh. The Qur'an states also that he followed the Way of Nuh.

Peace and salutation to Nuh among the nations! Thus indeed do we reward those who do right. For he was one of our believing Servants. Then the rest we overwhelmed in the Flood. Verily among those who followed his Way was Ibrahim. (Surat as-Saaffat: 79-83)

At the time of the prophet Ibrahim, many people living on the Mesopotamian plains, and in Middle and East Anatolia were worshipping the heavens and the stars. Their most important god was "Sin", the moon-god. It was personified as a human with a long beard, wearing a dress carrying a moon on it in the shape of a crescent. In addition, these people made embossed pictures and sculptures of these gods and worshipped them. This was quite a widespread belief system which found appropriate soil for itself in the Near East and thus maintained its existence for a long time. People living in that region continued to worship these gods until around 600 AD. As a consequence of this belief, some constructions known as "ziggurats" which were used both as observatories and temples, were built in the region stretching from Mesopotamia to the interior of Anatolia and here some gods, primarily the moon-god "Sin", were worshipped.[12]

This way of belief, only discovered in archaeological excavations today, is to be found mentioned in the Qur'an. As mentioned in the Qur'an, Ibrahim rejected the worship of these deities and turned only to Allah, the one true God. In the Qur'an, Ibrahim's conduct is recounted as follows;

Lo! Ibrahim said to his father Azar: "Takest thou idols for gods? For I see thee and thy people in manifest error."
So also did We show Ibrahim the power and the laws of the heavens and the earth, that he might (with understanding) have certitude.
When the night covered him over, He saw a star: He said: "This is my Lord." But when it set, He said: "I love not those that set."
When he saw the moon rising in splendour, he said: "This is my Lord." But when the moon set, He said: "unless my Lord guide me, I shall surely be among those who go astray."
When he saw the sun rising in splendour, he said: "This is my Lord; this is the greatest (of all)." But when the sun set, he said: "O my people! I am indeed free from your (guilt) of giving partners to Allah.
For me, I have set my face, firmly and truly, towards Him Who created the heavens and the earth, and never shall I give partners to Allah." (Surat al-Anaam: 74-79)

In the Qur'an, the birthplace of Ibrahim and where he lived are not told in detail. But it is indicated that Ibrahim and Lut lived close to each other and were contemporaries, by the fact that the angels sent to the people of Lut came to Ibrahim, and announced to his wife the good news of a child, before going on to Lut.

An important issue about Ibrahim in the Qur'an, not mentioned in the Old Testament, is the construction of the Ka'bah. In the Qur'an, we are

At the time of the prophet Ibrahim, polytheistic religions were prevalent in the Mesopotamian region. The moon-god, "Sin", was one of t most important deities. Peopl made statues of those gods ar worshipped them. On the left Sin's statues are seen. The cre cent figure can be clearly seer on the statue's chest.

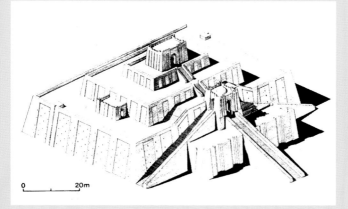

The ziggurats, which were used both as temples and astronomic observatories, were construction made with the most advanced techniques of the age. The stars the moon and the sun were the primary objects of worship, and therefore, the sky had great im- portance. Left and below are the important ziggurats of Mesopotamia.

told that the Ka'bah was constructed by Ibrahim and his son Isma'il. Today, the only thing known by historians about the past of the Ka'bah is that it is accepted to have been a sacred place since very old times. The placing of idols in the Ka'bah during the Age of Ignorance prior to the prophet Muhammad, is a consequence of the degeneration and distortion of the divine religion once revealed to Ibrahim.

Ibrahim According to the Old Testament

The Old Testament is probably the most detailed source on Ibrahim, even though much of what it relates may be unreliable. According to its account, Ibrahim was born around 1900 BC in the city of Ur, one of the most important cities of the time, which was located in the southeast of the Mesopotamia plains. When he was first born, Ibrahim was not named "Abraham", but "Abram". His name was changed by God (YHWH) afterwards.

One day, according to the Old Testament, God asked Abram to set out on a journey leaving his country and people, to go to an indefinite country and start a new community there. Abram, at the age of 75, listened to this call and set out on the road with his barren wife Sarai - who will later be known as "Sarah" which means princess - and his brother's son, Lut. While heading for the Chosen Land, they stayed at Harran for a while, and then continued on their journey. When they arrived in the land of Canaan promised to them by God, they were told that this place was specifically chosen for them and granted to them. When Abram turned ninety-nine years old, he made a covenant with God and his name was changed to Abraham. He died when he was one hundred and seventy-five years old and was buried in the cave of Machpelah close to the city of Hebron (el-Khalil) in the West Bank, today under occupation by Israel. This land bought by Ibrahim for a certain sum of money, was his and his family's first property in the Promised Land.

Ibrahim's Place of Birth According to the Old Testament

Where Ibrahim was born has always been an issue of debate. While Christians and Jews say that Ibrahim was born in South Mesopotamia, the prevalent thought in the Islamic world is that his place of birth is around Urfa-Harran. Some new finds show that the Jewish and Christian thesis does not reflect the truth completely.

Jews and Christians depend on the Old Testament for their assertion, because in it, Ibrahim is said to have been born in the city of Ur in South Mesopotamia. After Ibrahim was born and brought up in that city, he is said to have set out on the way to Egypt and to have reached Egypt at the end of a long journey in which he passed through the Harran region of Turkey.

However, a recently found manuscript of the Old Testament generated serious doubts about the validity of this information. In this Greek manuscript from the 3rd century BC, which is accepted to be the oldest copy of the Old Testament yet found, "Ur" is never mentioned. Today, many Old Testament researchers say that the word of "Ur" is inaccurate or a subsequent addition. This implies that Ibrahim was not born in the city of Ur, and may never have been to the Mesopotamian region in his life.

Besides, the names of some locations, and the regions they imply, change by time. In our day, the Mesopotamia plains generally refer to the south banks of the Iraqi land between the Euphrates and Tigris rivers. Yet two millennia before our day, Mesopotamia implied a region more northernly, even reaching as far as Harran, and stretching into presentday Turkish lands. Therefore, even if we accept that the expression "Mesopotamian plain" in the Old Testament is right, it would be misleading to think that the Mesopotamia of two millennia earlier and the Mesopotamia of today are exactly the same places.

Even if there are serious doubts and disagreements on the city of Ur being Ibrahim's birthplace, there is a common agreement on the fact that Harran and its environs region was the place where Ibrahim lived. Moreover, a short research made in the Old Testament itself yields some information supporting the view that Ibrahim's place of birth was Harran. For instance, in the Old Testament, the region of Harran is designated as the "Aram region" (Genesis, 11:31 and 28:10). It is stated that those who came from Ibrahim's family are "sons of an Arami" (Deuteronomy, 26:5). The identification of Ibrahim as an Arami shows that he led his life in this region.

In the Islamic sources, there is a strong evidence that Ibrahim's place of birth is Harran and Urfa. In Urfa, which is called the "city of Prophets", there are many stories and legends about Ibrahim.

Why was the Old Testament Altered?

The Old Testament and the Qur'an seem almost to describe two different prophets called Abraham and Ibrahim. In the Qur'an, Ibrahim is sent to an idolatrous people as a messenger. His people worship the heavens, stars, the moon and various idols. He struggles against his people, tries to get them turn away from their superstitious beliefs, and inevitably stirs up the enmity of his whole community including his father.

Actually, none of these are mentioned in the Old Testament. The throwing of Ibrahim into the fire, his breaking his community's idols are not mentioned in the Old Testament. Ibrahim is in general depicted as the ancestor of the Jews in the Old Testament. It is evident that this view in the Old Testament was taken by the chiefs of the Jewish community seeking to bring the concept of "'race'" to the foreground. The Jews believe that they are a people eternally chosen by God and rendered superior. They deliberately and willingly altered their Divine Book and made additions and deletions in accordance with this belief. This is why Ibrahim is merely depicted as the ancestor of the Jews in the Old Testament.

Christians who believe in the Old Testament, think that Ibrahim is the ancestor of the Jews, but with only one difference: according to Christians, Ibrahim is not a Jew but a Christian. The Christians, who did not heed the concept of race as much as Jews, took this stand and it is one of the causes of disagreement and struggle between the two religions. Allah brings the following explanation of these arguments in the Qur'an:

Ye People of the Book! Why dispute ye about Ibrahim, when the Law and the Gospel Were not revealed Till after him? Have ye no understanding? Ah! Ye are those who fell to disputing (Even) in matters of which ye had some knowledge! but why dispute ye in matters of which ye have no knowledge? It is Allah Who knows, and ye who know not! Ibrahim was not a Jew nor yet a Christian; but he was true in Faith, and bowed his will to Allah's (Which is Islam), and he joined not gods with Allah.

Without doubt, among men, the nearest of kin to Ibrahim, are those who follow him, as are also this Prophet and those who believe: And Allah is the Protector of those who have faith. (Surah Aal-e-Imran: 65-68)

In the Qur'an, very differently from what is written in the old Testament, Ibrahim is a person who warned his people so that they might fear Allah and who struggled against them for this end. Starting from his youth, he warned his people, who worshipped idols, to give up this practice. His people reacted to Ibrahim by attempting to kill him. Having escaped from the wickedness of his people, Ibrahim finally emigrated.

Chapter 3

The People of Lut and The City which was Turned Upside Down

The people of Lut rejected (his) warning. We sent against them a violent Tornado with showers of stones, (which destroyed them), except Lut's household: them We delivered by early Dawn,- As a Grace from Us: thus do We reward those who give thanks. And (Lut) did warn them of Our Punishment, but they disputed about the Warning. (Surat al-Qamar: 33-36)

L ut lived at the same time as Ibrahim. Lut was sent as a messenger to one of Ibrahim's neighbouring communities. These people, as the Qur'an tells us, practiced a perversion unknown to the world up to then, namely sodomy. When Lut told them to give up this perversion and brought them Allah's warning, they denied him, refused his prophethood, and carried on with their perversion. In the end, these people were destroyed by a dreadful disaster.

The city where Lut resided is referred to as Sodom in the Old Testament. Being situated at the north of the Red Sea, this community is understood to have been destroyed just as it is written in the Qur'an. Archaeological studies reveal that the city is located in the area of the Dead Sea which stretches along the Israel-Jordan border.

Before examining the remains of this disaster, let's see why the people of Lut were punished in this fashion. The Qur'an tells how Lut warned his people and what they said in reply;

The people of Lut rejected the messengers. Behold, their brother Lut said to them: "Will ye not fear (Allah)? I am to you a messenger worthy of all trust. So fear Allah and obey me. No reward do I ask of you for it: my reward is only from the lord of the Worlds. Of all the creatures in the world, will ye approach males, And leave those whom Allah has created for you to be your mates? Nay, ye are a people transgressing (all limits)!"

They said: "If thou desist not, O Lut! thou wilt assuredly be cast out!"

He said: "I do detest your doings." (Surat ash-Shuara: 160-168)

The people of Lut threatened him in response to his inviting them to the right way. His people detested him because of his showing them the right way, and wanted to banish both him and the other believers beside him. In other verses, the event is told as follows;

We also (sent) Lut: He said to his people: "Do ye commit lewdness such as no people in creation (ever) committed before you? For ye practise your lusts on men in preference to women : ye are indeed a people transgressing beyond bounds."

And his people gave no answer but this: they said, "Drive them out of your city: these are indeed men who want to be clean and pure!" (Surat al-Araf: 80-82)

Lut called his people to an obvious truth and warned them explicitly, but his people did not heed any warnings whatsoever and continued to reject Lut and to deny the penalty of which he told them.

And (remember) Lut: "Behold" he said to his people: "Ye do commit lewdness, such as no people in Creation (ever) committed before you. Do ye indeed approach men, and cut off the highway? And practise wickedness (even) in your councils?" But his people gave no answer but this: they said: "Bring us the Wrath of Allah if thou tellest the truth." (Surat al-Ankaboot: 28-29)

Receiving the above answer from his people, Lut asked for the help of Allah,

He said: "O my Lord! help Thou me against people who do mischief!" (Surat al-Ankaboot: 30)

"O my Lord! deliver me and my family from such things as they do!" (Surat ash-Shuara: 169)

Upon Lut's prayer, Allah sent two angels in the form of men. These angels visited Ibrahim before coming to Lut. Giving Ibrahim the good news that his wife would give birth to an infant, the messengers explained the reason of their being sent: the insolent people of Lut were to be destroyed.

(Ibrahim) said: "And what, O ye Messengers, is your errand (now)?" They said, "We have been sent to a people (deep) in sin; To bring on, on them, (a shower of) stones of clay (brimstone), Marked as from thy Lord for those who trespass beyond bounds." (Surat adh-Dhariyat: 31-34)

Excepting the adherents of Lut: them we are certainly (charged) to save (from harm) - All - Except his wife, who, We have ascertained, will be among those who will lag behind. (Surat al-Hijr: 59-60)

After leaving Ibrahim's company, the angels, who were sent as messengers, came to Lut. Not having met the messengers before, Lut first worried, but then calmed down after talking to them;

When Our messengers came to Lut, he was grieved on their account and felt himself powerless (to protect) them. He said: "This is a distressful day." (Surah Hud: 77)

He said: "Ye appear to be uncommon folk." They said: "Yea, we have come to thee to accomplish that of which they doubt. We have brought to thee that which is inevitably due, and assuredly we tell the truth. Then travel by night with thy household, when a portion of the night (yet remains), and do thou bring up the rear: let no one amongst you look back, but pass on whither ye are ordered." And We made known this decree to him, that the last remnants of those (sinners) should be cut off by the morning. (Surat al-Hijr: 62-66)

Meanwhile, his people had learned that Lut had visitors. They did not hesitate to approach these visitors perversely as they had approached others before. They encircled the house. Being afraid for his visitors, Lut addressed his people as follows;

Lut said: "These are my guests: disgrace me not: But fear Allah, and shame me not." (Surat al-Hijr: 68-69)

The people of Lut retorted;

They said: "Did we not forbid thee (to speak) for all and sundry?" (Surat al-Hijr: 70)

Thinking that he and his visitors subjected to evil treatment, Lut said:

"Would that I had power to suppress you or that I could betake myself to some powerful support." (Surah Hud: 80)

His "visitors" reminded him that they were the messengers of Allah and said;

(The Messengers) said: "O Lut! We are Messengers from thy Lord! By no means shall they reach thee! now travel with thy family while yet a part of the night remains, and let not any of you look back: but thy wife (will remain behind): To her will happen what happens to the people. Morning is their time appointed: Is not the morning nigh?" (Surah Hud: 81)

When the perversity of the city people reached its fullest extent, Allah saved Lut by means of the angels. In the morning, his people were destroyed by the disaster of which Lut had informed them in advance.

And they even sought to snatch away his guests from him, but We blinded their eyes. (They heard:) "Now taste ye My Wrath and My Warning." Early on the morrow an abiding Punishment seized them. (Surat al-Qamar: 37-38)

The verses describe the destruction of this people as follows;

But the (mighty) Blast overtook them before morning, And We turned (the cities) upside down, and rained down on them brimstones hard as baked clay. Behold! in this are Signs for those who by tokens do understand. And the (cities were) right on the high-road. (Surat al-Hijr: 73-76)

When Our Decree issued, We turned (the cities) upside down, and rained down on them brimstones hard as baked clay, spread, layer on layer,- Marked as from thy Lord: Nor are they ever far from those who do wrong! (Surah Hud: 82-83)

But the rest We destroyed utterly. We rained down on them a shower (of brimstone): and evil was the shower on those who were admonished (but heeded not)! : Verily in this is a Sign: but most of them do not believe. And verily thy Lord is He, the Exalted in Might, Most Merciful.(Surat ash-Shuara: 172-175)

When the people were destroyed, only Lut and the believers, who were only as many as one "household", were saved. Lut's wife did not believe either and she was also destroyed.

We also (sent) Lut: He said to his people: "Do ye commit lewdness such as no people in creation (ever) committed before you?
For ye practise your lusts on men in preference to women : ye are indeed a people transgressing beyond bounds."
And his people gave no answer but this: they said, "Drive them out of your city: these are indeed men who want to be clean and pure!"

But we saved him and his family, except his wife: she was of those who legged behind.

And we rained down on them a shower (of brimstone): Then see what was the end of those who indulged in sin and crime! (Surat al-Araf: 80-84)

Thus, Prophet Lut was saved along with the believers and his family with the exception of his wife. As described in the Old Testament, he emigrated with Ibrahim. As for the perverted people, they were destroyed and their dwellings were razed to the ground.

"The Obvious Signs" in the Lake of Lut

The 82nd verse of Surah Hud clearly states the kind of disaster that befell the people of Lut. "When Our Decree issued, We turned (the cities) upside down, and rained down on them brimstones hard as baked clay, spread, layer on layer"

The statement of "turning (the cities) upside down" implies that the region was totally destroyed by a violent earthquake. Accordingly, The Lake of Lut, where the destruction took place, bears "obvious" evidence of such a disaster.

We quote German archaeologist Werner Keller as follows;

Together with the base of this mighty fissure, which runs precisely through this area, the Vale of Siddim, including Sodom and Gomorrah, plunged one day into the abyss. Their destruction came about through a great earthquake which was probably accompanied by explosions, lightning, issue of natural gas and general conflagration. [13]

As a matter of fact, the Lake of Lut, or the Dead Sea as it is otherwise known, is located right on the top of an active seismic region, that is, an earthquake zone:

The base of the dead sea is located with a tectonic rooted downfall. This valley is located in a tension stretching between the Taberiye Lake in the north, and mid of Arabah Valley in the south.[14]

The event was expressed as "we rained down on them brimstones hard as baked clay, spread, layer on layer" in the last part of the verse. This is in all probability meant to be the volcanic explosion that took place on the

Jerusalem

Dead Sea

PEOPLE OF LUT

A satellite photograph of the region where the people of Lut lived.

banks of the Lake of Lut, and because of which the rocks and stones that erupted were in a "baked form". (The same event is related in the 173rd verse of Surat ash-Shuara as "We rained down on them a shower (of brimstone): and evil was the shower on those who were admonished (but heeded not)!")

In relation to this subject, Werner Keller writes;

The subsidence released volcanic forces that had been lying dormant deep down along the whole length of the fracture. In the upper valley of the Jordan near Bashan there are still towering craters of extinct volcanoes; great stretches of lava and deep layers of basalt have been deposited on the limestone surface.[15]

These lava and basalt layers constitute the greatest evidence that a volcanic explosion and earthquake had once taken place here. The catastro-

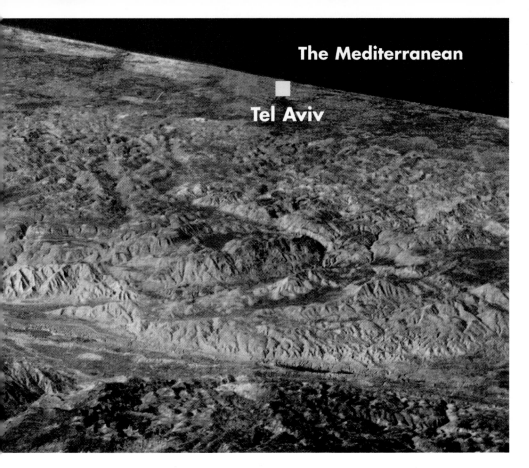

phe depicted in the following expression as "we rained down on them brimstones hard as baked clay, spread, layer on layer" in the Qur'an most probably points to this volcanic explosion, and Allah knows best. The expression "When Our Decree issued, We turned (the cities) upside down" which occurs in the same verse, must be referring to the earthquake which caused volcanoes to erupt over the surface of the earth with devastating impact, and to the fissures and debris brought by it, and only Allah knows the truth of it.

The "obvious signs" conveyed by the Lake of Lut are indeed very interesting. In general, the events which are related in the Qur'an take place in the Middle East, the Arabian Peninsula and Egypt. Right in the middle of these lands, is the Lake of Lut. The Lake of Lut, as well as the incidents that have taken place around it, deserves attention geologically. The Lake is approximately 400 metres below the surface of the Mediterranean. Since the deepest place in the Lake is 400 metres, the bottom of the Lake is 800

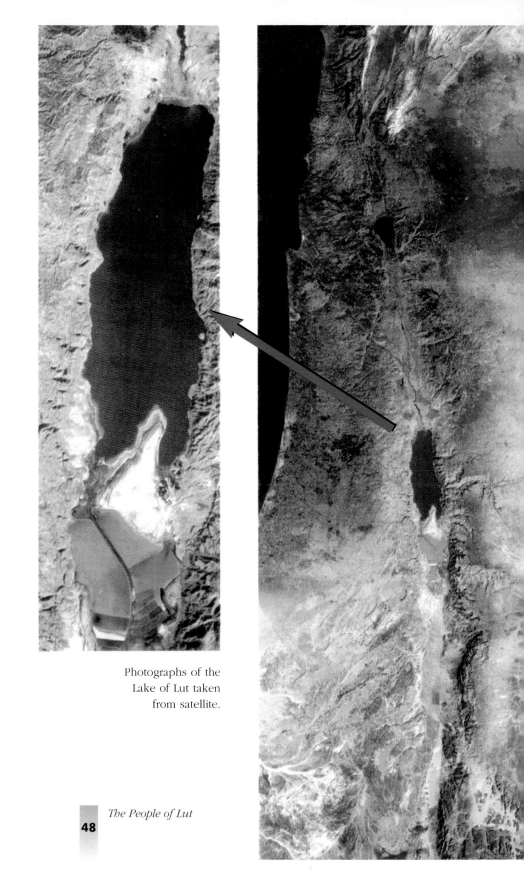

Photographs of the
Lake of Lut taken
from satellite.

The Lake of Lut, or Dead Sea as differently called.

metres below the surface of the Mediterranean. This is the lowest point on the earth. In other areas which are lower than sea level, the depth is at most 100 metres. Another property of the Lake of Lut is that the salt content of its water is very high, the density being nearly 30 %. Because of this, no living organism, such as fish or moss, can survive in this lake. This is why the Lake of Lut is called the "Dead Sea" in Western literature.

The incident of Lut's people, which is recounted in the Qur'an, occurred around 1800 BC according to estimates. Based on his archaeological and geological researches, the German researcher Werner Keller noted that the cities of Sodom and Gomorrah were in fact located in the Siddim Valley which was the region at the furthest and lowest end of the Lake of Lut, and that there were once big and widely inhabited sites in those regions.

The most interesting structural characteristic of the Lake of Lut is an evidence showing how the disaster incidence recounted in the Qur'an took place:

On the eastern shore of the Dead Sea the peninsula of el-Lisan protrudes like a tongue far into the water. El-Lisan means "the tongue" in Arabic. Unseen from the land the ground falls away here under the surface of the water at a prodigious angle, dividing the sea into two parts. To the right of

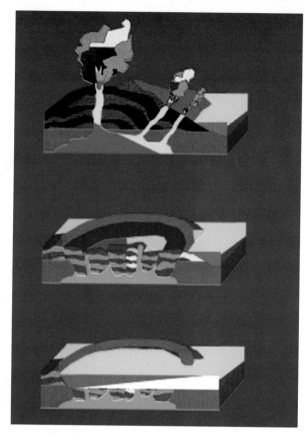

On the left:
an illustration
showing the
volcanic
eruption and
the collapse that
followed it, which
caused the whole
people to
disappear.

Page across: a
distant view of
the Lake of Lut

the peninsula the ground slopes sharply down to a depth of 1200 feet. On
the left of the peninsula the water remains remarkably shallow. Soundings
taken in the last few years established depths of only fifty to sixty feet. That
extraordinary shallow part of the Dead Sea, from the peninsula el-Lisan to
the southernmost tip, was the Vale of Siddim.[16]

Werner Keller noted that this shallow part, which was discovered to
have formed subsequently, was the outcome of the aforementioned earthquake and the massive collapse this earthquake had caused. This was the
place where Sodom and Gomorrah were situated, that is, where Lut's people lived.

Once, it was possible to cross this region by walking. However, now,
the Vale of Siddim, where Sodom and Gomorrah were once situated, is
covered by the flat surface of the lower part of the Dead Sea. The collapse
of the base as a result of the dreadful catastrophe that came to pass in the
beginning of the 2nd millennium BC, caused salt water from the north to
flow into this recently formed cavity and filled the basin with salty water.

verhead view of
ountains around
the Lake of Lut.

The traces of the Lake of Lut are visible… When one takes a rowing boat across the Lake of Lut to the southernmost point, if the sun is shining in the right direction, one sees something quite fantastic. Some distance from the shore and clearly visible under the surface of the water, there are the outlines of the forests which the extraordinarily high salt content of the Dead Sea preserved. The trunks and roots in the shimmering green water are very ancient. The Siddim valley, where these trees were once in blossom green foliage covered their twigs and branches, was one of the most beautiful locations in the region.

The mechanical aspect of the disaster that befell people of Lut is revealed by the researches of the geologists. These reveal that the earthquake which destroyed the people of Lut came about in consequence of quite a long crack in the earth (a fault line), along the 190 kilometres distance making up the bed of the River Sheri'at. River Sheri'at makes a fall of 180 metres in total. Both this and the fact that the Lake of Lut is 400 metres below sea level are two important pieces of evidence showing that an enormous geological event has taken place here.

Some of the remains of the city, which had slipped into the lake, were found on the banks of the lake. These remains showed that the people of Lut had quite a high standard of life

The destruction of the people of Lut has inspired many painters. An example is given above.

The interesting structure of River of Sheri'at and the Lake of Lut make up only a small part of the crack or split passing from this region of the earth. The condition and length of this crack have only recently been discovered.

The fault starts from the outskirts of Mount Taurus, stretches to the southern shores of the Lake of Lut and proceeds over the Arabian desert to the Gulf of Aqaba and continues across the Red Sea, ending up in Africa. Along the length of it, strong volcanic activities are observed. Black basalt and lava exist in the Galilee Mountains in Israel, high plain regions of Jordan, the Gulf of Aqaba and other areas nearby.

All these remains and geographical evidences show that a catastrophic geological event took place in the Lake of Lut. Werner Keller writes,

> Together with the base of this mighty fissure, which runs precisely through this area, the Vale of Siddim, including Sodom and Gomorrah, plunged one day into the abyss. Their destruction came about through a great earthquake which was probably accompanied by explosions, lightning, issue of natural gas and general conflagration. The subsidence released volcanic

forces that had been lying dormant deep down along the whole length of the fracture. In the upper valley of the Jordan near Bashan there are still towering craters of extinct volcanoes; great stretches of lava and deep layers of basalt have been deposited on the limestone surface.[17]

National Geographic makes the following comment on December 1957; The mount of Sodom, a barren wasteland, rises sharply above the dead sea. No one has ever found the destroyed cities of Sodom and Gomorrah, but scholars believe that they stood in the Vale of Siddim across from these cliffs. Possibly flood waters of the Dead Sea engulfed them following an earthquake.[18]

Pompeii Had a Similar End

The Qur'an tells us in the following verses that there is no change in Allah's laws;

They swore their strongest oaths by Allah that if a warner came to them, they would follow his guidance better than any (other) of the Peoples: But when a warner came to them, it has only increased their flight (from righteousness) - On account of their arrogance in the land and their plotting of Evil, but the plotting of Evil will hem in only the authors thereof. Now are they but looking for the way the ancients were dealt with? But no change wilt thou find in Allah's way (of dealing): no turning off wilt thou find in Allah's way (of dealing). (Surat al-Fatir: 42-43)

Yes, "no change will be found in Allah's way (rules)". Everybody, who stands against His laws and rebels against Him, is subject to the same divine law. Pompeii, the symbol of the degeneration of the Roman Empire, was also involved in sexual perversity. Its end was similar to that of the people of Lut.

The destruction of Pompeii came by means of the eruption of the volcano Vesuvius.

The volcano Vesuvius is the symbol of Italy, primarily the city of Naples. Remaining silent for the last two millennia, Vesuvius is named the "Mountain of Warning". It is not without cause that Vesuvius is known as such. The disaster that befell Sodom and Gomorrah is very similar to the disaster that destroyed Pompeii.

Above is a picture representing the luxury and prosperity of the city of Pompeii before the disaster.

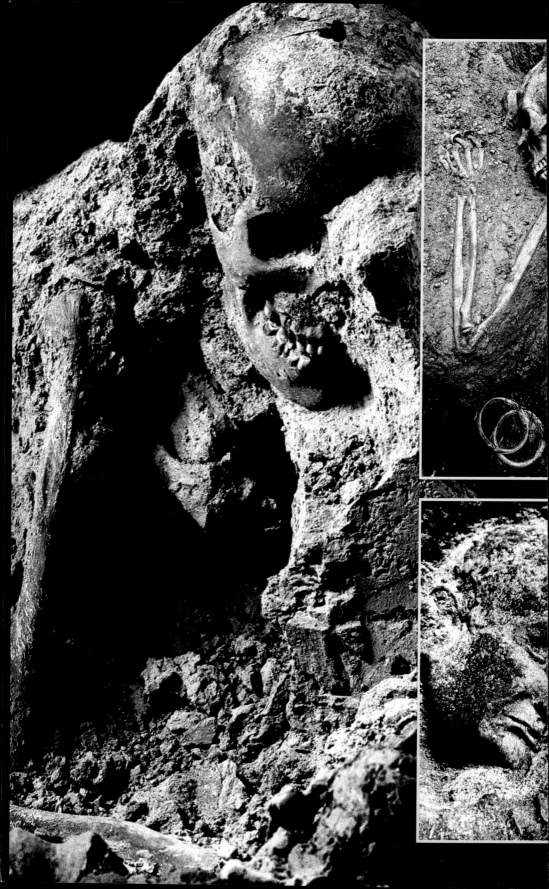

To the right of Vesuvius lies Naples and to the east lies Pompeii. The lava and ash of a huge volcanic eruption, that happened two millennia ago, caught the inhabitants of that city. The disaster happened so suddenly that everything in the town was caught in the middle of its everyday life and remains today exactly as it was two millennia ago. It is as if the time had been frozen.

The removal of Pompeii from the face of the earth by such a disaster was not purposeless. The historical record shows that the city was exactly a center of dissipation and perversity. The city was marked by a rise in prostitution to such an extent that even the number of brothels was not known. Male organs in their original sizes were hung on the doors of the brothels. According to this tradition, rooted in Mithraic belief, sexual organs and sexual intercourse should not be hidden but displayed openly.

But the lava of Vesuvius wiped the whole city off the map in a single moment. The most interesting aspect of the event is that nobody escaped despite the terrible violence of the eruption of Vesuvius. It is almost like they did not even notice the catastrophe, as if they were charmed. A family eating their meal were petrified right at that moment. Numerous petrified couples were found in the act of intercourse. The most interesting thing is that there were couples

On the next page
are petrified
corpses unearthed
in excavations
made in Pompeii.

of the same sex and couples of young boys and girls. The faces of some of the petrified human corpses unearthed from Pompeii were unharmed. The general expression on those faces was bewilderment.

Here lies the most incomprehensible aspect of the calamity. How did thousands of people wait to be caught by death without seeing and hearing anything?

This aspect of the event shows that the disappearance of Pompeii was similar to the destructive events mentioned in the Qur'an, because the Qur'an particularly points to "sudden annihilation" while relating these events. For example, the "inhabitants of the city" described in Surah Ya-seen died all at once in a single moment. The situation is told as follows in the 29th. verse of the surah;

> It was no more than a single mighty Blast, and behold! they were (like ashes) quenched and silent.

In the 31st verse of Surat al-Qamar, again the "instantaneous annihilation" is emphasised when the destruction of Thamud is recounted;

> For We sent against them a single Mighty Blast, and they became like the dry stubble used by one who pens cattle.

Other examples of petrified human corpses uncovered among the remains of Pompeii.

Some other examples of petrified human corpses uncovered at Pompeii. The picture on the left is a very good example of how instantanous the disaster was.

The death of the people of Pompeii took place instantaneously as just as the events recounted in the above verses.

Despite all these, things have not changed much where Pompeii once stood. The districts of Naples where debauchery prevails do not fall short of those licentious districts of Pompeii. The Island of Capri is a base where homosexuals and nudists reside. The Island of Capri is represented as a "Homosexual paradise" in tourist commercials. Not only on Capri and in Italy, but in nearly all the world, a similar moral degeneration is at work and people insist on not learning from the awful experiences of past peoples.

Chapter 4

The People of 'Ad and Ubar, the "Atlantis of the Sands"

And the 'Ad, they were destroyed by a furious Wind, exceedingly violent;
He made it rage against them seven nights and eight days in succession: so that thou couldst see the (whole) people lying prostrate in its (path),
as they had been roots of hollow palm-trees tumbled down!
Then seest thou any of them left surviving?
(Surat al-Haaqqa: 6-8)

A nother people who were destroyed and who are mentioned in various Surah of the Qur'an is 'Ad, who are mentioned after the people of Nuh. Being sent to 'Ad, Hud summoned his people, just like all the other prophets had done, to believe in Allah without ascribing partners to Him and to obey him, the prophet of that time. The people reacted to Hud with animosity. They accused him of imprudence, untruthfulness, and attempting to change the system their ancestors had established.

In Surah Hud, all that passed between Hud and his people is told in detail;

> To the Ad People (We sent) Hud, one of their own brethren. He said: "O my people! worship Allah! ye have no other god but Him. (Your other gods) ye do nothing but invent!
>
> O my people! I ask of you no reward for this (Message). My reward is from none but Him who created me: Will ye not then understand?
>
> And O my people! Ask forgiveness of your Lord, and turn to Him (in repentance): He will send you the skies pouring abundant rain, and add strength

to your strength: so turn ye not back in sin!"

They said: "O Hud! No Clear (Sign) that hast thou brought us, and we are not the ones to desert our gods on thy word! Nor shall we believe in thee! We say nothing but that (perhaps) some of our gods may have seized thee with imbecility."

He said: "I call Allah to witness, and do ye bear witness, that I am free from the sin of ascribing, to Him, Other gods as partners! so scheme (your worst) against me, all of you, and give me no respite. I put my trust in Allah, My Lord and your Lord! There is not a moving creature, but He hath grasp of its fore-lock. Verily, it is my Lord that is on a straight Path.

If ye turn away,- I (at least) have conveyed the Message with which I was sent to you. My Lord will make another people to succeed you, and you will not harm Him in the least. For my Lord hath care and watch over all things."

So when Our decree issued, We saved Hud and those who believed with him, by (special) Grace from Ourselves: We saved them from a severe penalty.

Such were the Ad People: they rejected the Signs of their Lord and Cherisher; disobeyed His messengers; And followed the command of every powerful, obstinate transgressor.

And they were pursued by a Curse in this life - and on the Day of Judgment. Ah! Behold! for the 'Ad rejected their Lord and Cherisher! Ah! Behold! removed (from sight) were 'Ad the people of Hud! (Surah Hud: 50-60)

Another Surah mentioning 'Ad is Surat ash-Shuara. In this Surah, some characteristics of 'Ad are emphasised. According to this, 'Ad were a people who "build a landmark on every high place" , and its members "get for themselves fine buildings in the hope of living therein (for ever)". Besides, they did mischief and behaved brutally. When Hud warned his people, they commented that his words were "a customary device of the ancients". They were very confident that nothing would happen to them;

The 'Ad (people) rejected the messengers.

Behold, their brother Hud said to them: "Will ye not fear (Allah)?

I am to you a messenger worthy of all trust:

So fear Allah and obey me. No reward do I ask of you for it: my reward is only from the Lord of the Worlds.

Do ye build a landmark on every high place to amuse yourselves? And do ye get for yourselves fine buildings in the hope of living therein (for ever)? And when ye exert your strong hand, do ye do it like men of absolute power?

Now fear Allah, and obey me.

Yea, fear Him Who has bestowed on you freely all that ye know.

Freely has He bestowed on you cattle and sons,

And Gardens and Springs.

Truly I fear for you the Penalty of a Great Day."

They said: "It is the same to us whether thou admonish us or be not among (our) admonishers!

This is no other than a customary device of the ancients, And we are not the ones to receive Pains and Penalties!"

So they rejected him, and We destroyed them. Verily in this is a Sign: but most of them do not believe.

And verily thy Lord is He, the Exalted in Might, Most Merciful. (Surat ash-Shuara: 123-140)

The people who showed animosity to Hud and rebelled against Allah, were indeed destroyed. A horrible sandstorm annihilated 'Ad as if they had "never existed".

The Archaeological Finds of the City of Iram

At the beginning of 1990, there appeared press-releases in the well-known newspapers of the world declaring "Fabled Lost Arabian city found", "Arabian city of Legend found", "The Atlantis of the Sands, Ubar". What rendered this archaeological find more intriguing was the fact that this city was also referred to in the Qur'an. Many people who, since then, thought that 'Ad recounted in the Qur'an were a legend or that their location could never be found, could not conceal their astonishment at this discovery. The discovery of this city, which was only mentioned in oral stories of Bedouins, awoke great interest and curiosity.

It was Nicholas Clapp, an amateur archaeologist, who found this legendary city mentioned in the Qur'an.[19] Being an Arabophile and a winning documentary film maker, Clapp had come across a very interesting book during his research on Arabian history. This book was *Arabia Felix* written by the English researcher Bertram Thomas in 1932. *Arabia Felix* was the

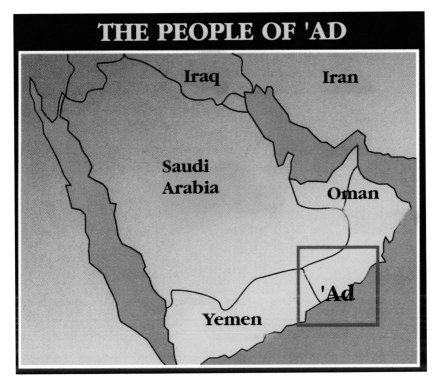

THE PEOPLE OF 'AD

Iraq

Iran

Saudi
Arabia

Oman

'Ad

Yemen

The remains of the city of Ubar, where 'Ad lived, were found somewhere near to the coasts of Oman

Roman designation for the southern part of the Arabian Peninsula which today includes Yemen and much of Oman. The Greeks called this area "Eudaimon Arabia" and medieval Arab scholars called it "Al-Yaman as-Saida". [20]

All of these names mean "Fortunate Arabia", because the people living in that region in old times were known to be the most fortunate people of their time. Well, what was the reason for such a designation?

Their good fortune was in part due to their strategic location - serving as middlemen in the spice trade between India and places north of the Arabian peninsula. Besides, the people living in this region produced and distributed "frankincense", an aromatic resin from rare trees. Being highly favoured by the ancient communities, this plant was used as a fumigant in various religious rites. In those times, the plant was at least as valuable as gold.

**Many works of art and monuments of high civilisation were once erect-
ed in Ubar in accordance with the Qur'an's account. Today, only the**

Excavations made in Ubar

The English researcher Thomas described these "lucky" tribes at length and claimed that he found the traces of an ancient city founded by one of these tribes.[21]This was the city known as "Ubar" by the bedouins. In one of the trips he made to the region, the bedouins living in the desert had shown him well-worn tracks and stated that these tracks led toward the ancient city of Ubar. Thomas, who showed great interest in the subject died before being able to complete his research.

Clapp, who examined what the English researcher Thomas wrote, was convinced of the existence of the lost city described in the book. Without losing much time, he started his research.

Clapp tried two ways to prove the existence of Ubar. First, he found the tracks which the Bedoins said existed. He applied to NASA to provide the satellite images of the area. After a long struggle, he succeeded in per-suading the authorities to take the pictures of the region.[22]

Clapp went on to study the ancient manuscripts and maps in the Huntington library in California. His aim was to find a map of the region. After a short research, he found one. What he found was a map drawn by

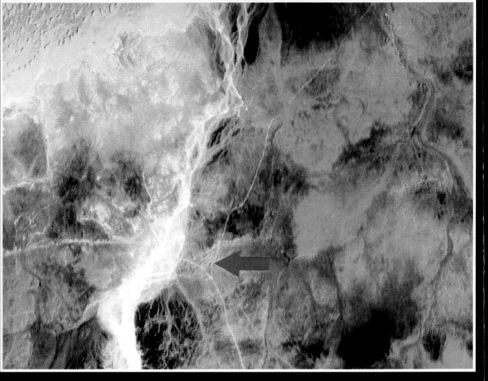

The location of the city of 'Ad was discovered by photographs taken from the Space Shuttle. On the photograph, the place where caravan trails intersect is marked, and it points towards Ubar.

1. Ubar, could only be seen from space before excavations were made.
2. A city 12 metres below the sands was uncovered by excavations.

the Greek-Egyptian geographer Ptolemy. In the map was shown the location of an old city found in the region and the ways that led to this city.

Meanwhile, he received the news that the pictures had been taken by NASA. In the pictures, some caravan trails became visible which were difficult to identify with the naked eye, but could only be seen as a whole from the sky. Comparing these pictures with the old map he had in hand, Clapp finally reached the conclusion he was looking for: the trails in the old map corresponded with the trails in the pictures taken from the satellite. The final destination of these trails was a broad site understood to have once been a city.

Finally, the location of the legendary city which had been subject of the stories told orally by the bedouins was discovered. After a short while, excavations began and remains of an old city started to be uncovered under the sands. Thus, this lost city was described as "the Atlantis of the Sands, Ubar".

Well, what was it that proved this city to be the city of the people of 'Ad mentioned in the Qur'an?

Right from the moment remains started to be unearthed, it was understood that this ruined city belonged to 'Ad and Iram's pillars mentioned in the Qur'an, because among the structures unearthed were the towers particularly referred to in the Qur'an. A member of the research team leading the excavation, Dr. Zarins said that since the towers were alleged to be the distinctive feature of Ubar, and since Iram was mentioned as having towers or pillars, this then was the strongest proof so far that the site they had unearthed was Iram, the city of 'Ad described in the Qur'an. The Qur'an mentions Iram as follows;

Seest thou not how thy Lord dealt with the 'Ad (people),-
Of the (city of) Iram, with lofty pillars,
The like of which were not produced in (all) the land? (Surat al-Fajr: 6-8)

The People of 'Ad

So far, we have seen that Ubar could possibly be the city of Iram mentioned in the Qur'an. According to the Qur'an, the inhabitants of the city did not listen to the prophet Hud, who had brought a message to them and who warned them, and so they perished.

The identity of 'Ad who found the city of Iram has also created much debate. In historical records, there is no mention of a people having such a developed culture or of the civilisation they established. It might be thought quite strange that the name of such a people is not found in historical records.

On the other hand, it shouldn't be so surprising not to come across the presence of these people in the records and archives of old civilisations. The reason for that is that these people lived in South Arabia, which was a region distant from other people living in the Mesopotamia region and the Middle East, and which only had a restricted relationship with them. It was a common situation for a state, which is scarcely known, not to be recorded in the historical records. On the other hand, it is possible to hear stories among people in the Middle East about 'Ad.

The most important reason why 'Ad have not been mentioned in the written records is that written communication was not common in the region at that time. Therefore, it is possible to think that 'Ad founded a civilisation but this civilisation had not been mentioned in the historical records of those other civilisations that kept documentation. If this culture had existed a little longer, maybe much more would be known about these people in our day.

There is no written record of 'Ad, but it is possible to find important information about their "descendants" and to have an idea about 'Ad in the light of this information.

Hadramites, the Descendants of 'Ad

The first place to be looked at while searching for the traces of a probable civilisation established by 'Ad or their descendants, is South Yemen, where "The Atlantis of the Sands, Ubar" is found and which is referred to as "Fortunate Arabia". In South Yemen, four peoples have existed before our time who are named "Fortunate Arabs" by the Greeks. These are the Hadramites, Sabaeans, Minaeans and Qatabaeans. These four peoples reigned for a while together in territories close to each other.

Many contemporary scientists say that 'Ad entered into a period of transformation and then re-appeared on the stage of history. Dr. Mikail H. Rahman, a researcher at the University of Ohio, believes that 'Ad are the ancestors of the Hadramites, one of the four peoples who lived in South Yemen. Appearing around 500 BC, The Hadramites are the least known among the people called "Fortunate Arabs". These people reigned over the region of South Yemen for a very long time and disappeared totally in 240 AD at the end of a long period of decline.

The name of Hadrami hints that those may be the descendants of 'Ad. The Greek writer Pliny, living at the 3rd century BC, referred to this tribe as "Adramitai" - meaning the Hadrami.[23] The termination of the Greek name is a noun-suffix, the noun being "Adram" which immediately suggests that it is a possible corruption of "Ad-i Iram" mentioned in the Qur'an.

The Greek geographer Ptolemy (87-150 AD) shows the south of the Arabian Peninsula as the place where the people called "Adramitai" lived. This region has been known by the name of "Hadhramaut" until recently. The capital city of the Hadrami State, Shabwah, was situated at the west of the Hadhramaut Valley. According to many old legends, the tomb of the prophet Hud, who was sent as a messenger to 'Ad, is in Hadhramaut .

Another factor which tends to confirm the thought that the Hadramites are a continuation of 'Ad, is their wealth. The Greeks defined the Hadramites as the "richest race in the world...". Historical records say that the Hadramites had gone very far in the agriculture of "frankincense", one of the most valuable plants of the time. They had found new areas of usage for the plant and widened its usage. The agricultural production of the Hadramites was much higher than production of this plant in our day.

What has been found in the excavations made in Shabwah, which is known to have been the capital city of the Hadramites, is very interesting. In these excavations which started in 1975, it was extremely difficult for archaeologists to reach the remains of the city due to the deep sand dunes. The finds obtained by the end of the excavations were astonishing; because the uncovered ancient city was one of the most overwhelmingly interesting found until then. The walled town that was revealed was of a larger extent than of any other ancient Yemeni site and its palace was remarked to be a truly magnificent building

Doubtless, it was very logical to suppose that the Hadramites had inherited this architectural superiority from their forerunners, 'Ad. Hud said to the people of 'Ad while warning them;

> Do ye build a landmark on every high place to amuse yourselves? And do ye get for yourselves fine buildings in the hope of living therein (for ever)? (Surat ash-Shuara: 128-129)

Another interesting characteristic of the buildings found at Shabwah was the elaborate columns. The columns that were at Shabwah seemed to be quite unique in being round and arranged in a circular portico, whereas all other sites in Yemen so far had been found to have square monolithic columns. The people of Shabwah must have inherited the architectural style of their ancestors, 'Ad. Photius, a Greek Byzantine Patriarch of Constantinople in the 9th. Century AD, made vast research on the Southern Arabs and their commercial activities because he had access to the old Greek manuscripts no longer extant in our day, and particularly the book of Agatharachides (132 BC), Concerning the Erythraean (Red) Sea. Photius said in one of his articles; "It is said that they (South Arabians) have built many columns covered in gold or made of silver. Spaces between these columns are remarkable to behold" [24]

Although the above statement of Photius does not directly refer to the Hadramites, it does give an idea of the affluence and building prowess of the people living in the region. Greek classical writers Pliny and Strabo describe these cities as "adorned with beautiful temples and palaces".

When we think that the owners of these cities were the descendants of 'Ad, it is clearly understood why the Qur'an defines the home of 'Ad as "the city of Iram, with lofty pillars" (Surat al-Fajr: 7).

The Springs and the Gardens of 'Ad

Today, the landscape that someone, who travels to Southern Arabia, would most frequently come across is the vast desert. Most of the places, with the exception of the cities and regions that have been later afforested, are covered with sand. These deserts have been there for hundreds and maybe thousands of years.

But in the Qur'an, an interesting information is given in one of the verses recounting 'Ad. While warning his people, Prophet Hud draws their attention to the springs and gardens with which Allah had endowed them;

> Now fear Allah, and obey me. Yea, fear Him Who has bestowed on you freely all that ye know. Freely has He bestowed on you cattle and sons,- And Gardens and Springs. Truly I fear for you the Penalty of a Great Day. (Surat ash-Shuara: 131-135)

But as we have noted before, Ubar, which has been identified with the city of Iram, and any other place which is likely to have been the residence of 'Ad, is totally covered with desert today. So, why did Hud use such an expression while warning his people?

The answer is hidden in the climatic changes of history. Historical records reveal that these areas which have turned into desert now, had once been very productive and green lands. A great part of the region was covered with green areas and springs as told in the Qur'an, less than a few thousand years ago, and the people of the region made use of these endowments. The forests softened the harsh climate of the region and made it more habitable. Deserts existed, but did not cover such a vast area as today.

In Southern Arabia, important clues have been acquired in the regions where 'Ad lived, which could cast a light upon this subject. These show that the inhabitants of that region used a highly developed irrigation system. This irrigation most probably served a single purpose: agriculture. In those regions, which are not appropriate for life today, people once cultivated the land.

Satellite imaging had also revealed an extensive system of ancient canals and dams used in irrigation around Ramlat as Sab'atayan which is estimated to have been able to support 200,000 people in the associated cities.[25] As Doe, one of the researchers conducting the research, said; "So fertile was the area around Ma'rib, that one might conceive that the whole region between Ma'rib and Hadhramaut was once under cultivation." [26]

The Greek classical writer Pliny had described this region as being very fertile, and mist-covered with forested mountains, rivers and unbroken tracts of forests. In the inscriptions found in some ancient temples close to Shabwah, the capital city of the Hadramites, it was written that animals were hunted in this region and that some were sacrificed. All these reveal that this region was once covered with fertile lands as well as desert.

The speed with which the desert can encroach can be seen in some recent research done by the Smithsonian Institute in Pakistan where an area known to be fertile in the middle ages has turned into sandy desert, with dunes 6 metres high, the desert being found to expand on average 6 inches a day. At this speed, the sands can swallow even the highest buildings, and cover them as if they had never existed. Thus excavations at Timna in Yemen in the 1950's have been almost completely covered up again. The Egyptian pyramids were also entirely under sands once and were only brought to light after very long-lasting excavations. Briefly, it is very clear that regions known to be desert today could have had different appearances in the past.

How were 'Ad ruined?

In the Qur'an, 'Ad are said to have perished through a "furious wind". In the verses, it is mentioned that this furious wind lasted for seven nights and eight days and destroyed 'Ad totally.

> The 'Ad (people) (too) rejected (Truth): then how terrible was My Penalty and My Warning? For We sent against them a furious wind, on a Day of violent Disaster, Plucking out men as if they were roots of palm-trees torn up (from the ground). (Surat al-Qamar: 18-20)

> And the 'Ad, they were destroyed by a furious Wind, exceedingly violent. He made it rage against them seven nights and eight days in succession: so that thou couldst see the (whole) people lying prostrate in its (path), as they had been roots of hollow palm-trees tumbled down! (Surat al-Haaqqa: 6-7)

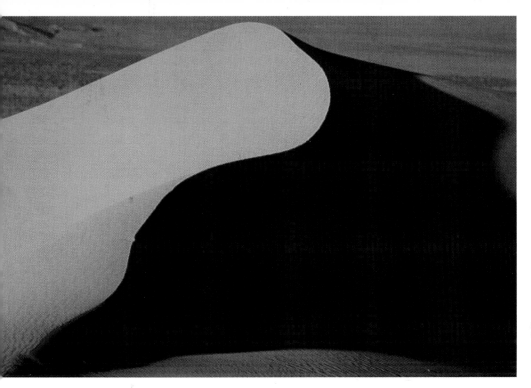

Today, the region where 'Ad lived is full of sand dunes.

Though warned previously, the people had paid no attention to the warnings whatsoever and continuously refused their messengers. They were in such delusion that they could not even understand what was happening when they saw the destruction approaching them and continued with their denial.

Then, when they saw the (Penalty in the shape of) a cloud traversing the sky, coming to meet their valleys, they said, "This cloud will give us rain!". Nay, it is the (Calamity) ye were asking to be hastened!- A wind wherein is a Grievous Penalty! (Surat al-Ahqaf : 24)

In the verse, it is stated that the people saw the cloud that would bring them calamity, but could not understand what it was and thought that it was a rain cloud. This is an important indication as to how the calamity was as it drew near to the people, because a cyclone proceeding along whipping up the desert sand also seems like a rain cloud from a distance. It is possible that 'Ad were deceived by this appearance and did not notice the calamity. Doe gives a description of these sand storms (which seems to be from personal experience); "The first sign (of a dust or sandstorm) is an approaching wall of dust-laden air which may be several thousand feet in height lifted by the strong rising currents and stirred by a fairly strong wind." [27]

Thought to be the remains of 'Ad, "the Atlantis of the Sands, Ubar" has been recovered from under a layer of sand metres thick. It seems that the furious wind lasting for "seven nights and eight days" by the Qur'an's description, accumulated tons of sand on top of the city and buried people under the earth alive. Excavations made in Ubar point to the same possibility. The French magazine, *Ça M'Interesse* states the same as follows "Ubar was buried under a sand of 12 metres thickness as a result of a storm"[28]

The most important evidence showing that 'Ad were buried by a sand storm, is the word "ahqaf" used in the Qur'an to signify the location of 'Ad. The description used in the 21st verse of Surat al-Ahqaf is as follows;

> Mention (Hud) one of 'Ad's (own) brethren: Behold, he warned his people about the winding Sand-tracts: but there have been warners before him and after him: "Worship ye none other than Allah: Truly I fear for you the Penalty of a Mighty Day."

The excavations made in Ubar where the remains of a city was recovered from under a layer of sand metres thick. In this region, it is very well known that a catastrophic sand storm can cause a huge amount of sand to accumulate in a very short time. This can happen suddenly, and in a very unexpected way.

Ahqaf means "sand dunes" in Arabic and it is the plural form of the word "hiqf" which means a "sand dune". This shows that 'Ad lived in a region full of "sand dunes", which provided the most logical ground possible for the fact that they were buried by a sand storm. According to one interpretation, ahqaf lost its meaning of "sand hills" and became the name of the region in south Yemen where 'Ad lived. This does not change the fact that the root of this word is sand dunes, but just shows that this word has since become peculiar to this area because of the abundant sand dunes in the region.

The destruction that befell 'Ad from a sand storm which "plucked out men as if they were roots of palm-trees torn up (from the ground)", must have annihilated the entire people in a very short time, people who were until then living by cultivating fertile lands and building dams and irrigation channels for themselves. All of the fertile and cultivated fields, irrigation canals and dams of the community living there were covered by sand, and the whole city and its inhabitants were buried alive under the sand. After the people were destroyed, desert spread there in time and covered them leaving no trace.

As a consequence, it can be said that historical and archaeological finds indicate that 'Ad and the city of Iram existed and were destroyed as described in the Qur'an. By later research, the remains of these people have been recovered from the sands.

What one should do in looking at those remains buried in the sands, is to take warning just as the Qur'an stresses. The Qur'an states that 'Ad went astray of the right path because of their arrogance and said "Who is superior to us in strength?". In the rest of the verse, it is said "Did they not see that Allah, Who created them, was superior to them in strength?" (Surah Fussilat: 15)

What a person has to do is bear this unchangeable fact in mind all the time and understand that the greatest and the most honoured is always Allah and that one can only prosper by adoring Him.

The Thamud (also) rejected (their) Warners. For they said:
"What! a man! a Solitary one from among ourselves! shall we follow such
a one? Truly should we then be straying in mind, and mad!"
"Is it that the Message is sent to him,
of all people amongst us? Nay, he is a liar, an insolent one!"
Ah! they will know on the morrow, which is the liar,
the insolent one! (Surat al-Qamar:, 23-26)

As stated in the Qur'an, Thamud rejected the warnings of Allah just as 'Ad did and perished in consequence. Today, as a result of archaeological and historical studies, many previously unknown things have been brought into daylight, such as the location where Thamud lived, the houses they made and their life-styles. The Thamud mentioned in the Qur'an, are a historic fact confirmed by many archaeological finds today.

Before looking at these archaeological finds related to Thamud, it is useful to examine the story in the Qur'an and to look over the struggle of these people with their prophet. As the Qur'an is a book addressing all times, Thamud's denial of the warnings coming to them is an incident which is itself a warning to people of all ages.

The prophet Salih's conveyance of the message

In the Qur'an, it is mentioned that Salih was sent to Thamud to warn them. Salih was a recognised person within Thamud society. His people, who did not expect him to proclaim the religion of truth, were surprised by his calling on them to abandon their deviation. Their first reaction was to slander and condemn him;

> To the Thamud People (We sent) Salih, one of their own brethren. He said: "O my people! Worship Allah: ye have no other god but Him. It is He Who hath produced you from the earth and settled you therein: then ask forgiveness of Him, and turn to Him (in repentance): for my Lord is (always) near, ready to answer."
> They said: "O Salih! thou hast been of us! a centre of our hopes hitherto! dost thou (now) forbid us the worship of what our fathers worshipped? But we are really in suspicious (disquieting) doubt as to that to which thou invitest us." (Surah Hud: 61-62)

A small part of the community complied with Salih's call, but most of them did not accept what he told. The leaders of the community in particular denied Salih and took an antagonistic stand towards him. They tried to impede those who believed Salih and tried to oppress them. They were enraged at Salih, because he called them to worship Allah. This rage was not specific only to Thamud; Thamud were repeating the mistake made by the people of Nuh and by Ad' who had lived before them. This is why the Qur'an refers to these three communities as follows,

> Has not the story reached you, (O people!), of those who (went) before you? - of the people of Prophet Nuh, and 'Ad, and Thamud? - And of those who (came) after them? None knows them but Allah. To them came messengers with Clear (Signs); but they put their hands up to their mouths, and said: "We do deny (the mission) on which ye have been sent, and we are really in suspicious (disquieting) doubt as to that to which ye invite us." (Surah Ibrahim: 9)

Despite the prophet Salih's warnings, the people still went on overcome by doubts. But still, there was a group who believed in the prophethood of Salih – and those were the ones who were saved along with Salih when the great catastrophe came. The leaders of the community tried to oppress the group believing in Salih;

> The leaders of the arrogant party among his people said to those who were reckoned powerless - those among them who believed: "know ye indeed that Salih is a messenger from his Lord?" They said: "We do indeed believe in the revelation which hath been sent through him." The Arrogant party said: "For our part, we reject what ye believe in." (Surat al-Araf: 75-76)

Thamud still continued in doubt regarding Allah and the prophethood of Salih. Moreover, a certain group openly denied Salih. A group among those who rejected faith - supposedly in the name of Allah - made plans to kill Salih.

They said: "Ill omen do we augur from thee and those that are with thee". He said: "Your ill omen is with Allah; yea, ye are a people under trial." There were in the city nine men of a family, who made mischief in the land, and would not reform. They said: "Swear a mutual oath by Allah that we shall make a secret night attack on him and his people, and that we shall then say to his heir (when he seeks vengeance): 'We were not present at the slaughter of his people, and we are positively telling the truth.'" They plotted and planned, but We too planned, even while they perceived it not. (Surat an-Naml: 47-50)

To see whether his people would follow Allah's commands, Salih showed them a female camel as a trial. To see whether they would obey him or not, he told his people to share their water with this female camel and not to harm her. His people reacted by killing the camel. In Surat ash-Shuara, the events are described as follows;

The Thamud (people) rejected the messengers.
Behold, their brother Salih said to them: "Will you not fear (Allah)?
I am to you a messenger worthy of all trust.
So fear Allah, and obey me.
No reward do I ask of you for it: my reward is only from the Lord of the Worlds.
Will ye be left secure, in (the enjoyment of) all that ye have here?
Gardens and Springs,
And corn-fields and date-palms with spathes near breaking (with the weight of fruit)?
And ye carve houses out of (rocky) mountains with great skill.
But fear Allah and obey me;
And follow not the bidding of those who are extravagant,
Who make mischief in the land, and mend not (their ways)."
They said: "Thou art only one of those bewitched!
Thou art no more than a mortal like us: then bring us a Sign, if thou tellest the truth!"
He said: "Here is a she-camel: she has a right of watering, and ye have a

right of watering, (severally) on a day appointed.

Touch her not with harm, lest the Penalty of a Great Day seize you."

But they ham-strung her: then did they become full of regrets. (Surat ash-Shuara: 141-157)

The prophet Salih's struggle with his people is told as follows in Surat al-Qamar:

The Thamud (also) rejected (their) Warners.

For they said: "What! a man! a Solitary one from among ourselves! shall we follow such a one? Truly should we then be straying in mind, and mad!

Is it that the Message is sent to him, of all people amongst us? Nay, he is a liar, an insolent one!"

Ah! they will know on the morrow, which is the liar, the insolent one!

For We will send the she-camel by way of trial for them. So watch them, (O Salih), and possess thyself in patience!

And tell them that the water is to be divided between them: Each one's right to drink being brought forward (by suitable turns).

But they called to their companion, and he took a sword in hand, and ham-strung (her). (Surat al-Qamar: 23-29)

The fact that they were not punished at that very moment, increased the insolence of these people more. They attacked Salih, criticised him and accused him of being a liar .

Then they ham-strung the she-camel, and insolently defied the order of their Lord, saying: "O Salih! bring about thy threats, if thou art a messenger (of Allah)!" (Surat al-Araf: 77)

Allah rendered the plans and stratagems of the unbelievers feeble and saved Salih from the hands of those who wanted to do him harm. After this event, seeing that he had proclaimed the message to his people in many different ways and that still nobody took the advice to heart, Salih told his people that they would be destroyed in three days;

But they did ham-string her. So he said: "Enjoy yourselves in your homes for three days: (Then will be your ruin): (Behold) there a promise not to be belied!" (Surah Hud: 65)

Sure enough, three days later, Salih's warning came true and the Thamud were destroyed.

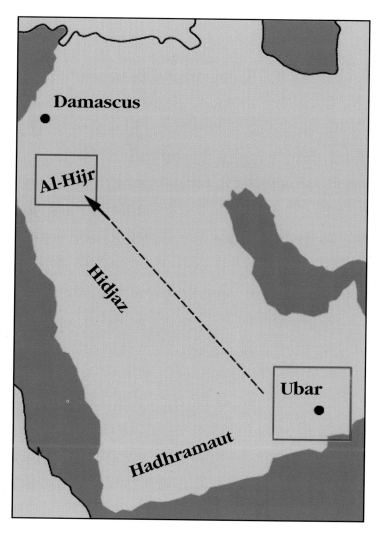

From the Qur'an, it is understood that Thamud were the descendants of 'Ad. In agreement with that, archaeological finds show that the roots of Thamud, who lived in the north of the Arabian Peninsula, go back to South Arabia where 'Ad had once lived.

The (mighty) Blast overtook the wrong-doers, and they lay prostrate in their homes before the morning - As if they had never dwelt and flourished there. Ah! Behold! For the Thamud rejected their Lord and Cherisher! Ah! Behold! removed (from sight) were the Thamud! (Surah Hud: 67-68)

Archaeological Finds about Thamud

Of those peoples mentioned in the Qur'an, Thamud are some of the people about whom we have the most extensive knowledge today. Historical resources reveal that a people called Thamud indeed existed.

The community of al-Hijr mentioned in the Qur'an are thought to be the same people as Thamud. The other name of Thamud is Ashab al-Hijr. So, the word "Thamud" is the name of a people, while the city of al-Hijr is one of those cities founded by these people. The Greek geographer Pliny's descriptions agree with this. Pliny wrote that Domatha and Hegra were the locations where Thamud resided, and this latter makes up the city of Hijr today.[29]

The oldest sources known referring to Thamud, are the victory annals of the Babylonian King, Sargon II (8th Century BC), who defeated these people in a campaign in northern Arabia. The Greeks also refer to this people as "Tamudaei", i.e. "Thamud", in the writings of Aristo, Ptolemy, and Pliny.[30] Before the Prophet Muhammad, approximately between 400-600 AD, they totally disappeared.

In the Qur'an, 'Ad and Thamud are always mentioned together. Moreover, the verses advise Thamud to take warning from the destruction of 'Ad. This shows that Thamud had detailed information on 'Ad.

> To the Thamud people (We sent) Salih, one of their own brethren: He said: "O my people! worship Allah: ye have no other god but Him" (Surat al-Araf: 73)

> "And remember how He made you inheritors after the 'Ad people and gave you habitations in the land: ye build for yourselves palaces and castles in (open) plains, and care out homes in the mountains; so bring to remembrance the benefits (ye have received) from Allah, and refrain from evil and mischief on the earth." (Surat al-Araf: 74)

As understood from the verse, there is a relationship between 'Ad and Thamud, and 'Ad may even have been a part of Thamud's history and culture. Salih ordered Thamud to remember the example of 'Ad and to take warning from them.

'Ad were shown the example of Nuh's people who had lived before them. Just as 'Ad had a historical importance for Thamud, Nuh's people also had an historical importance for 'Ad. These people were aware of each other and possibly came from the same lineage.

However, the places where 'Ad and Thamud lived were geographically quite far from each other. There does not seem to be a relationship

The Nabataeans, which was an Arab tribe, had established a kingdom in the Rum Valley in Jordan. In this place, also called the Valley of Petra, it is possible to see the best examples of the stone-carving work of these people. Also in the Qur'an, Thamud are mentioned with their mastery of masonry. However, today, what is left of both of these communities are some remains that give us an idea of the art of that time. In the pictures, various examples of the stone-carving work in Petra Valley are seen.

And remember how He made you inheritors after the 'Ad people and gave you habitations in the land: ye build for yourselves palaces and castles in (open) plains, and carve out homes in the mountains; so bring to remembrance the benefits (ye have received) from Allah, and refrain from evil and mischief on the earth.
(Surat al-Araf: 74)

between these two communities; so why is it said in the verse addressed to Thamud for them to remember 'Ad?

The answer reveals itself after a short investigation. The geographical distance between the 'Ad and Thamud is deceptive. Historical sources reveal that there is indeed a very strong connection between Thamud and 'Ad. Thamud knew 'Ad, because these two peoples most likely came from the same origin. *Britannica Micropaedia* writes about these people as follows under the title of "Thamud".

> In ancient Arabia, tribe or group of tribes that seem to have been prominent. Although the Thamud probably originated in Southern Arabia, a large group apparently moved northward at an early date, traditionally settling on to the slopes of Jabal (Mount) Athlab. Recent archaeological work has revealed numerous Thamudic rock writings and pictures not only on Jabal Athlab, but also throughout Central Arabia.[31]

A script graphically similar to the Smaitic alpabet (called Thamudic) has been found in southern Arabia and up throughout the Hidjaz.[32] The script was first identified in a region in north central Yemen that is known as Thamud, which is bound to the north by the Rub'al Khali, to the south by the Hadramaut and to the west by Shabwah.

Before, we had seen that 'Ad were a people living in South Arabia. It is very significant that some remains of Thamud were found in the region where 'Ad had lived, especially around the region where the Hadramites, the descendants of 'Ad, lived and where their capital city stood. This situation explains the 'Ad-Thamud relationship noted in the Qur'an. This relationship is explained as follows in the prophet Salih's words when he said that Thamud came to replace 'Ad.

> To the Thamud people (We sent) Salih, one of their own brethren:
> He said: "O my people! worship Allah: ye have no other god but Him..." (Surat al-Araf : 73)
> And remember how He made you inheritors after the 'Ad people and gave you habitations in the land (Surat al-Araf: 74)

Briefly, Thamud paid the price for not obeying their messenger and they were destroyed. The buildings they had built and the works of art they had produced could not protect them from punishment. Thamud were destroyed with a terrible punishment just like all the other peoples both before and after them who denied the Truth.

Chapter 6

Fir'awn Who Was Drowned

*(Deeds) after the manner of the people of Fir'awn and those
before them: They treated as false the Signs of their Lord: so We
destroyed them for their crimes, and We drowned the people of
Fir'awn: for they were all oppressors and wrong-doers.
(Surat al-Anfal: 54)*

Ancient Egyptian Civilisation, along with other city states established in Mesopotamia at the same time, is known to be one of the
oldest civilisations in the world and it is recognised to have be-
en an organised state with the most advanced social order of its age. The
facts that they discovered writing around the 3rd millennium BC and used
it, that they made use of the river Nile and were protected against dangers
abroad on account of the natural setting of the country, greatly contributed
to the Egyptians improving their civilisation.

But this "civilised" society was one in which "the reign of pharaohs" prevailed, which is the system of infidelity mentioned in the clearest and most
straightforward way in the Qur'an. They puffed up with pride, turned asi-
de and blasphemed. In the end, neither their advanced civilisations, their
social and political orders, nor their military successes could save them
from being destroyed.

The Authority of the Pharaohs

The Egyptian civilisation was based on the fertility of the River Nile.
Egyptians had settled in the Nile valley due to the abundant water of this
river, and because they could cultivate the land with the water supplied by

the river without being dependent on rainy seasons. The historian Ernst H. Gombrich states in his writing that Africa is very hot and sometimes it does not rain there at all for months. For this reason, many areas in this huge continent are extremely dry. Those parts of the continent are covered with vast desert. Both sides of the River Nile are also covered with deserts, and it hardly rains in Egypt. But in this country, rain is not needed so much, because the River Nile runs right down the middle of the whole country. [33]

So, whoever has control of the River Nile, which is of such great importance, is also able to control Egypt's biggest source of commerce and agriculture. The pharaohs were able to establish their dominance over Egypt in this way.

The narrow and vertical form of the Nile valley did not allow residential units situated around the river to expand much, and therefore Egyptians formed a civilisation made up of small-scaled towns and villages instead of big cities. This factor also fortified the dominance of the pharaohs over their people.

King Menes is known to be the first Egyptian Pharaoh who united the whole of ancient Egypt, for the first time in history, in a united state around the 3rd millennium BC. In fact, the term "pharaoh" originally referred to the palace where the Egyptian king lived, but in time, it became the title of Egyptian kings. This is why the kings, who were rulers of Old Egypt started to be called "pharaohs".

Being owners, administrators and rulers of the whole state and its lands, these pharaohs were accepted as reflections of the biggest god in the distorted polytheistic religion of old Egypt. The administration of Egyptian lands, their division, their income, in short, all the estates, services and production within the country's borders were managed on behalf of the pharaoh.

The absolutism in the regime had furnished the pharaoh ruling the country with such a power that he could have anything he wished. Right at the establishment of the first dynasty, at the time of Menes who became the first King of Egypt by uniting Upper and Lower Egypt, the River Nile started to be delivered to the public through canals. Beside that, production was taken under control and the entire production of goods and services were assigned to the king. The king distributed and shared these goods and services in the proportions his people needed. It was not hard for the kings, who had established such a power in the region, to reduce the people to submission. The King of Egypt, or with his future name, the pharaoh, was looked upon as a holy being who held great power and met all the needs of his people: and he was transformed into a god. The Pharaohs definitely believed in time that they were indeed gods.

Some of the words the pharaoh mentioned in the Qur'an used during his conversation with Musa prove that they held this belief. He tried to intimidate Musa by saying "If thou dost put forward any god other than me, I will certainly put thee in prison!" (Surat ash-Shuara: 29), and he said to the people around him "no god do I know for you but myself" (Surat al-Qasas: 38). He said all this because he regarded himself as a god.

Religious Beliefs

According to the historian Herodotus, the Ancient Egyptians were the most "devout" people in the world. However, their religion was not the religion of Truth, but a perverse polytheistic one and they could not abandon their perverse religion because of their extreme conservatism.

The Ancient Egyptians were largely influenced by the natural environment in which they lived. The natural geography of Egypt protected the country against external attacks perfectly. Egypt was surrounded by deserts, mountainous lands and seas on all sides. Attacks likely to be made on the country had two possible routes and it was very simple for the Egyptians to defend those routes. The Egyptians remained isolated from the external world thanks to these natural factors. But passing centuries transformed this isolation into a dark bigotry. Thus the Egyptians acquired a viewpoint which was locked against new developments and novelties, and which was extremely conservative about their religion. The "religion of their ancestors" mentioned frequently in the Qur'an became their most important value.

The religious beliefs of the Egyptians were mainly based on serving their gods. The "intermediaries" between these gods and people were the priests who were among the leaders of the society. Dealing with magic and witchcraft, the priests made an important class whom the Pharaohs used in order to keep the people in submission.

This is why Fir'awn and his close circle turned their backs on Musa and Harun when they announced the Religion of Truth to them, by saying: "Hast thou come to us to turn us away from the ways we found our fathers following - in order that thou and thy brother may have greatness in the land? But not we shall believe in you!" (Surah Yunus: 78)

The religion of Ancient Egypt was divided into branches, the most important of which were the official religion of the state, the beliefs of the people and belief in life after death.

According to the state's official religion, the pharaoh was a holy being. He was a reflection of the people's gods on earth and his purpose was to dispense justice and protect them on earth.

The beliefs widespread among people were extremely complicated, and the elements in item which clashed with the state's official religion were oppressed by the reigns of the Pharaohs. Basically, they believed in many gods, and these gods were usually depicted as having animal heads on human bodies. But it was also possible to meet with local traditions which differed from region to region.

Life after death made up the most important part of Egyptian belief. They believed that the soul went on living after the body died. According to this, the souls of the dead were brought by particular angels to the God who was a Judge and forty-two other witness judges, a scale was set in the middle and the heart of the soul was weighed in this scale. Those with more goodness passed on to a beautiful setting and lived in happiness, those with more wickedness were sent to a place where they were subject to great torments. There, they were tormented throughout eternity by a strange creature called the "The Dead Eater".

The belief of the Egyptians in the Hereafter clearly shows a parallelism with the monotheistic belief and the religion of Truth. Even their belief in the hereafter alone proves that the religion of truth and the message had reached ancient Egyptian civilisation, but that this religion was later corrupted, and monotheism was turned into polytheism. It is already known that warners calling people to the unity of Allah and summoning them to be His slaves were sent in Egypt from time to time, as they were to all the earth's peoples at one time or another. One of these was the prophet Yusuf whose life is told in detail in the Qur'an. The history of Yusuf is also extremely important because it includes the arrival of the Children of Israel in Egypt and their settlement there.

On the other hand, in the historical resources, there are references to some Egyptians who invited people to monotheistic religions even before Musa. One of them is the most interesting pharaoh in the history of Egypt, that is, Amenhotep IV .

The Monotheistic Pharaoh Amenhotep IV

The Egyptian pharaohs were generally brutal, oppressive, belligerent and ruthless people. In general, they adopted the polytheistic religion of Egypt and deified themselves through this religion.

Amenhotep IV

But there is a pharaoh in Egyptian history who is very different from the others. This pharaoh defended belief in a single Creator and was subjected to great resistance by the priests of Ammon, who profited from the polytheistic religion, and some soldiers who supported them, and so he was finally killed. This pharaoh was Amenhotep IV who rose to power in the 14th Century BC.

When Amenhotep IV was enthroned in 1375 BC, he came across a conservatism and traditionalism which had been lingering for centuries. Until then, the structure of the society and the relations of the public with the royal palace had carried on without any change. The society kept all its doors firmly shut to all external events and religious innovations. This extreme conservatism, also remarked by ancient Greek travellers, was caused by the natural geographical conditions of Egypt as we have explained above.

Imposed on people by the pharaohs, the official religion required an unconditional faith in everything old and traditional. But Amenhotep IV did not adopt the official religion. The historian Ernst Gombrich writes;

He (Amenhotep IV) broke with many of the customs hallowed by an age-old tradition. He did not wish to pay homage to the many strangely shaped gods of his people. For him only one god was supreme, Aton, whom he worshipped and whom he had represented in the shape of the sun. He called himself Akhenaton, after his god, and he moved his court out of reach of the priests of the other gods, to a place which is now called El-Amarna[34]

After the death of his father, young Amenhotep IV was subjected to great pressure. This oppression was caused by the fact that he developed a religion based on monotheism by changing the traditional polytheistic religion of Egypt, and attempting to make radical changes in all fields. But

the leaders of Thebes did not allow him to convey the message of this religion. Amenhotep IV and his folk moved away from the city of Thebes
and settled in Tell-El-Amarna. Here, they established a new and modern
city named "Akh-et-aton". Amenhotep IV changed his name which meant
"Contentment of Amon" to Akh-en-aton, which meant "Submitting to Aton".
Amon was the name given to the greatest totem in Egyptian polytheism.
According to Amenhotep, Aton is the "creator of the heavens and the
earth", his equating the name with Allah.

Disturbed by these developments, the priests of Ammon wanted to
snatch Akhenaton's power by profiting from an economic crisis in the country. Akhenaton was finally killed by being poisoned by conspirators.
Succeeding pharaohs were careful to stay under the influence of the priests.

After Akhenaton, pharaohs with a military background came to power.
These again caused the old traditional polytheism to become widespread
and spent a considerable effort to return to the past. Nearly a century later, Ramses II, who was to have the longest rule in the history of Egypt,
came to the throne. According to many historians, Ramses was the pharaoh tormenting the Children of Israel and fighting against Musa.[35]

The Coming of the Prophet Musa

Because of their deep bigotry, the ancient Egyptians would not abandon their idolatrous beliefs. Some persons came to them who announced
the message of worshipping only Allah, but the people of Fir'awn always
turned back to their perverted beliefs. Finally, Musa was sent by Allah as
a messenger (rasul) to them, both because they had adopted a system of
falsehood contrary to the religion of truth, and also because they had enslaved the Children of Israel. Musa was instructed both to invite Egypt to
the religion of truth, and to save the Children of Israel from slavery and
show them the right way. In the Qur'an, it is stated;

> We rehearse to thee some of the story of Prophet Musa and Fir'awn in
> Truth, for people who believe. Truly Fir'awn elated himself in the land and
> broke up its people into sections, depressing a small group among them:

their sons he slew, but he kept alive their females: for he was indeed a maker of mischief. And We wished to be Gracious to those who were being depressed in the land, to make them leaders (in Faith) and make them heirs, to establish a firm place for them in the land, and to show Fir'awn, Haman, and their hosts, at their hands, the very things against which they were taking precautions. (Surat al-Qasas: 3-6)

Fir'awn wanted to prevent the Children of Israel increasing in number, by killing all new-born male babies. This was why, by inspiration from Allah, Musa's mother placed him in a basket and left him in the river. This was the way that led him into the palace of Fir'awn. In the Qur'an, the verses on the subject are as follows;

So We sent this inspiration to the mother of Musa: "Suckle (thy child), but when thou hast fears about him, cast him into the river, but fear not nor grieve: for We shall restore him to thee, and We shall make him one of Our messengers."

Then the people of Fir'awn picked him up (from the river): (It was intended) that (Musa) should be to them an adversary and a cause of sorrow: for Fir'awn and Haman and (all) their hosts were men of sin.

The wife of Fir'awn said: "(Here is) joy of the eye, for me and for thee: slay him not. It may be that he will be use to us, or we may adopt him as a son." And they perceived not (what they were doing)! (Surat al-Qasas: 7-9)

Fir'awn's wife prevented the murder of Musa and adopted him. This way, Musa spent his childhood in Fir'awn's palace. With the help of Allah, his own mother was brought to the palace as his wet-nurse.

When he had become an adult, one day Musa intervened when he saw one of the children of Israel being tormented by an Egyptian and he struck the Egyptian one blow upon which the Egyptian died. Despite the fact he was living in the palace of Fir'awn, and he had been adopted by the Queen, the chiefs of the city decided that his punishment was to be death. Hearing this, Musa ran away from Egypt and came to Madyan. At the end of the period he passed there, Allah spoke directly to him and Allah gave him the station of prophethood. He was ordered to return to Fir'awn and convey the message of Allah's religion to him.

The enslaved people whom Fir'awn wronged. Particularly in the age of the New Kingdom, minorities living in the country were set to work on massive construction projects. The Children of Israel were among those minorities. In the picture above top, the slaves who are seen working on the construction of a temple are most likely the Children of Israel. The picture below depicts technical preparations of slaves, again thought to be the Children of Israel, before setting to work on a construction project. The slaves are making bricks by boiling mud on fire, and preparing mortar.

Considered to be the pharaoh mentioned in the Qur'an according to many historians, Ramses II is seen killing some of the slaves he has captured. As these wall pictures also re-veal, the pharaohs had themselves idealised and depicted as strong warriors. They were presented as tall heroes with wide shoulders who could overcome a number of people at one time.

Above: Since the pharaohs saw themselves as divine beings, they tried to seem superior to all other people.

Next: War captives seized by the Egyptians are seen waiting for the execution of their death sentence.

Fir'awn's Palace

Musa and Harun went to Fir'awn in obedience to Allah's command and conveyed him the message of the religion of truth. They asked him to stop tormenting the Children of Israel and let them go with Musa and Harun. It was unacceptable to Fir'awn that Musa, whom he had kept near him for years and who most probably was to have been his successor on the throne, stood up to him and talked to him in this manner. For that reason, Fir'awn accused him of ingratitude;

(Fir'awn) said: "Did we not cherish thee as a child among us, and didst thou not stay in our midst many years of thy life? And thou didst a deed of thine which (thou knowest) thou didst, and thou art an ungrateful (wretch)!" (Surat ash-Shuara: 18-19)

Fir'awn was trying to play on Musa's sentiments and affect his conscience. It was as if he was saying that since it was he and his wife who had brought him up, it was Musa who should obey them. Moreover, Musa had killed an Egyptian. All these acts required heavy penalties according to the Egyptians. This emotional atmosphere which Fir'awn tried to create, was also directed at influencing the leaders of his people, so that they would also agree with Fir'awn.

On the other hand, the message of the religion of truth proclaimed by Musa undermined Fir'awn's power, and reduced him to the level of ordinary people. From then on, it would be revealed that he was not a god, and moreover he would be compelled to obey Musa. Besides, if he set the Children of Israel free, he would loose some important manpower and thus could fall in great distress.

For all these, Fir'awn did not even listen to what Musa said. He tried to make fun of him, and attempted to change the subject by asking meaningless questions. At the same time, he tried to represent Musa and Harun as anarchists and accuse them of being politically motivated. Finally, neither Fir'awn nor the leaders of the people within his close circle, except for the magicians, obeyed Musa and Harun. They did not follow the religion of truth shown to them. Therefore Allah first of all sent some disasters to them.

Ramses II is seen in his war chariot driving a big group of enemies. Just like many others, this is an imaginary scenario Fir'awn made his painters draw.

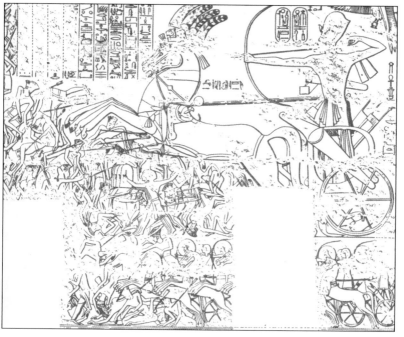

The War of Kadesh. This battle held between Ramses and the Hittites, was falsely passed on by Egyptian history as a great victory for Fir'awn. In fact, Fir'awn was saved from death at the last moment, and had to make peace.

The Disasters That Befell Fir'awn and His Close Circle

Fir'awn and his close circle were so deeply engaged in their polytheism and their idolatry, that is "the religion of their ancestors", that they never considered leaving it. Even two of the main miracles of Musa, his hand appearing white and his rod turning into snake, were not enough to make them move away from their superstitions. Moreover, they expressed this openly. They said "Whatever be the Signs thou bringest, to work therewith thy sorcery on us, we shall never believe in thee." (Surat al-Araf: 132)

Because of their conduct, Allah sent them a number of disasters as "separate miracles" to make them taste the torment in this world, before the eternal torment of the eternal world. The first of these was drought and scarcity of crops. In relation to the subject, it is written in the Qur'an: "We punished the people of Fir'awn with years (of droughts) and shortness of crops; that they might receive admonition." (Surat al-Araf: 130).

Egyptians had based their agricultural system on the River Nile and, therefore, they were not influenced by changes in natural conditions. But an unexpected disaster befell them because Fir'awn and his close friends were proud and arrogant towards Allah and denied His prophet. Most probably, for various reasons, the level of the River Nile sank a great deal and irrigation canals running off from the river did not carry enough water to agricultural areas. Extreme heat caused the crops to dry up. Thus, the disaster came on Fir'awn and his circle from a very unexpected direction, from the River Nile upon which they relied. This drought dismayed Fir'awn who previously used to address his people as follows "O my people! Does not the dominion of Egypt belong to me, (witness) these streams flowing underneath my (palace)? What! see ye not then?" (Surat az-Zukhruf: 51)

However, instead of "taking heed" as shown in the verses, they held all that had happened was because of ill fortune brought by Musa and the Children of Israel. They were overcome by such a conviction because of their superstitions and the religion of their ancestors. Because of this, they chose to suffer from great distress, but what befell them was not limited to these. This was just a beginning. Afterwards, Allah sent to them a series of disasters. These disasters are described as follows in the Qur'an;

> So We sent (plagues) on them: Wholesale death, Locusts, Lice, Frogs, and Blood: Signs openly self-explained: but they were steeped in arrogance - a people given to sin.(Surat al-Araf: 133)

These disasters Allah sent on Fir'awn and the people around him who also denied were also described in the Old Testament in agreement with the Qur'an:

> And there was blood throughout all the land of Egypt.(Exodus, 7:21)
> And if thou refuse to let [them] go, behold, I will smite all thy borders with frogs: And the river shall bring forth frogs abundantly, which shall go up and come into thine house, and into thy bedchamber, and upon thy bed, and into the house of thy servants, and upon thy people, and into thine ovens, and into thy kneadingtroughs. (Exodus, 8:2-3)
> And the LORD said unto Moses, "Say unto Aaron, Stretch out thy rod, and smite the dust of the land, that it may become lice throughout all the land of Egypt." (Exodus, 8:16)
> And the locusts went up over all the land of Egypt, and rested in all the coasts of Egypt: very grievous [were they]; before them there were no such locusts as they, neither after them shall be such. (Exodus, 10:14)
> Then the magicians said unto Pharaoh, This [is] the finger of God: and Pharaoh's heart was hardened, and he hearkened not unto them; as the LORD had said. (Exodus, 8:19)

Awful disasters kept happening to Fir'awn and his close circle. Some of these disasters were caused by the objects worshipped as gods by the idolatrous people. For example, the River Nile and frogs were sacred for them and had been deified by them. As they expected guidance from their "gods" and called for their help, Allah punished them through their own "gods" so that they could see their mistakes and pay for the wrongs they had done.

According to interpreters of the Old Testament, the "blood" was the turning of the River Nile into blood. This was explained as a metaphor for the River Nile's turning solid red. According to an interpretation, what gave the river this colour was a type of bacteria.

The Nile was the main source of life for the Egyptians. Any harm done to this source could mean death for the whole of Egypt. If the bacteria had covered the River Nile so fully as to turn it red, this would cause every living thing using this water to be infected by these bacteria.

Recent explanations of the cause for the red colouring of water has favoured protozoan, zooplankton, both salt - and fresh - water algal (phytoplankton) blooms, and dinoflagellates. All of these various blooms - plant, fungal or protozoan - deoxygenate water and produce noxious toxins for both fish and frogs.

Citing the Exodus account in the Bible, Patricia A. Tester of the National Marine Fisheries Service, writing in the Annals of the New York Academy of Science, noted that while fewer than 50 out of approximately 5,000 known phytoplankton species are toxic, those which possess toxins can be dangerous to aquatic life. In the same publication, Ewen C. D. Todd of Health Canada, referring to historic and prehistoric data, cited nearly two dozen examples of specific phytoplanktons causing various outbreaks throughout the world. W. W. Carmichael and I. R. Falconer listed diseases associated with fresh-water blue-green algae. Aquatic ecologist Joann M. Burkholder, of North Carolina State University, described a dinoflagellate, Pfiesteria piscimorte (found in estuary waters) that is capable of, as the species name implies, killing fish. [36]

In Fir'awn's time, this kind of chain of disasters appears to have occurred. According to this scenario, when the Nile was contaminated, fish also died, and the Egyptians were deprived of an important source of nutrition. Without predator fish, the frogs could initially breed freely in both ponds and the Nile and thus overpopulate the river, eventually escaping the anoxic, toxic, and putrefying environment by migrating to land, hence dying on land and decomposing along with the fish. The Nile and adjacent lands thus became fouled, and the waters dangerous to drink or to bathe in. Moreover, the extinction of frog species causes bugs such as locusts and lice to reproduce excessively.

Finally, no matter how the disasters took place, and what effect they left, neither Fir'awn, nor his people turned to Allah by paying heed, but they went on in their arrogance.

Fir'awn and his close circle were so hypocritical that they thought they could deceive Musa and thus, Allah. When the dreadful penalty fell upon them, they at once called for Musa and asked him to save them from it:

Every time the penalty fell on them, they said: "O Musa! on your behalf call on thy Lord in virtue of his promise to thee: If thou wilt remove the penalty from us, we shall truly believe in thee, and we shall send away the Children of Israel with thee." But every time We removed the penalty from them according to a fixed term which they had to fulfil.
Behold! they broke their word! (Surat al-Araf: 134-135)

Exodus from Egypt

Allah explained to Fir'awn and his close circle through Musa that which they had to take heed of, and thus warned them. In response, they rebelled and accused him of being possessed and untrue. Allah prepared a humiliating end for them. He revealed to Musa what was to happen.

By inspiration we told Musa: "Travel by night with my servants; for surely ye shall be pursued."
Then Fir'awn sent heralds to (all) the Cities,
(Saying): "These (Israelites) are but a small band,
And they are raging furiously against us;
But we are a multitude amply fore-warned."
So We expelled them from gardens, springs,
Treasures, and every kind of honourable position;
Thus it was, but We made the Children of Israel inheritors of such things.
So they pursued them at sunrise.
And when the two bodies saw each other, the people of Musa said: "We are sure to be overtaken." (Surat ash-Shuara: 52-61)

In such circumstances, when the Children of Israel thought that they were trapped, and Fir'awn's men thought that they were about to catch them, Musa said, never loosing faith in Allah's help: "By no means! my Lord is with me! Soon will He guide me!" (Surat ash-Shuara: 62)

At that moment, Allah saved Musa and the Children of Israel by dividing the sea. Fir'awn and his men were drowned under the waters which closed over them after the Children of Israel had safely crossed.

Then We told Musa by inspiration: "Strike the sea with thy rod." So it divided, and each separate part became like the huge, firm mass of a mountain.

And We made the other party approach thither.

We delivered Musa and all who were with him;

But We drowned the others. Verily in this is a Sign: but most of them do not believe. And verily thy Lord is He, the Exalted in Might, Most Merciful. (Surat ash-Shuara: 63-68)

Musa's rod had miraculous qualities. Allah had turned it into a snake in His first revelation to him, and then this same rod had turned into a snake again and swallowed the sorceries of Fir'awn's magicians. Now, Musa divided the sea with the same rod. This was one of the greatest miracles given to the prophet Musa.

Did the Incident Take Place on the Mediterranean Coasts of Egypt, or in the Red Sea?

There is no common agreement on the place where Musa divided the sea. Since no detail is given on the subject in the Qur'an, we cannot be sure of the correctness of any of the views on the subject. Some sources show the Mediterranean shores of Egypt as the place where the sea was divided. In the *Encyclopedia Judaica*, it is said;

The majority opinion today identifies the Red Sea of the Exodus with one of the lagoons on the shores of the Mediterranean[37]

David Ben Gurion said that the event could have taken place during the reign of Ramses II, possibly after the Kadesh defeat. In the Book of Exodus in the Old Testament, the event is said to have happened in Migdol and Baal-Zephon, which are located to the north of the delta[38]

This view is based on the Old Testament. In the translations of the Book of Exodus from the Old Testament, it is said that Fir'awn and his men were drowned in the Red Sea. But according to those who hold this view, the word translated as "The Red Sea" is in fact "The Sea of Reeds". The word is identified with the "Red Sea" in many sources, and used for that location. However, "The Sea of Reeds" is actually used to refer to the Mediterranean coast of Egypt. In the Old Testament, while mentioning the ro-

ute followed by Musa and those following him, the words Migdol and Baal-Zephon are mentioned, and these are located to
the north in the Nile Delta, on the shore of Egypt. The Sea of
Reeds, by implication, supports the possibility that the incident
may have happened on the Egyptian shores, because in this
region, in agreement with the meaning of the name, reeds are
produced thanks to the delta alluvions.

The Drowning of Fir'awn and His Men in the Sea

The Qur'an informs us about the most important aspects of
the event of the division of the Red Sea. According to the account of the Qur'an, Musa set out to leave Egypt with the
Children of Israel who obeyed him. However, Fir'awn could
not accept their departure without his permission. He and his
soldiers followed them "in insolence and spite" (Surah Yunus:
90). By the time Musa and the Children of Israel reached the
shore, Fir'awn and his soldiers had caught up with them. Some of the Children of Israel, who saw this, began to complain
to Musa. According to the Old Testament, they said to Musa

> We save thee in the body, that thou
> mayest be a sign to those who
> come after thee! but verily, many
> among mankind are heedless of
> Our Signs! (Surah Yunus: 92)

Fir'awn who was Drowned

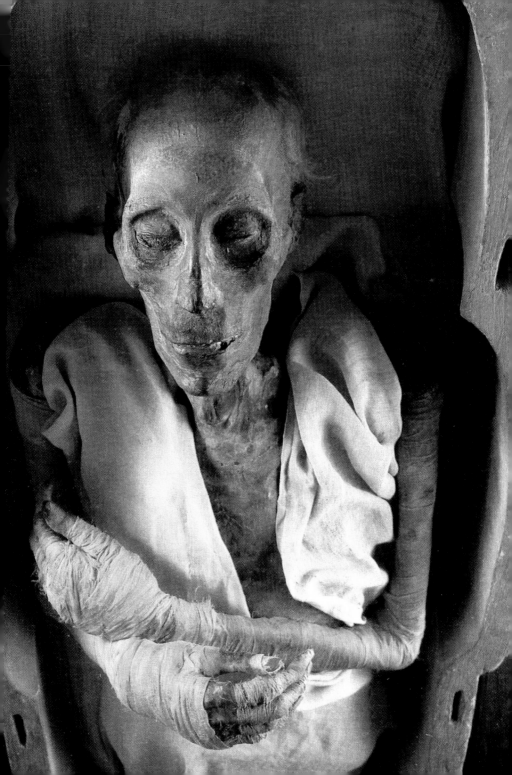

"why did you take us away from our homeland, there we were slaves but we could lead our lives, now we will die". This weakness of the community is also described in the Qur'an in the following verse: "And when the two bodies saw each other, the people of Musa said: 'We are sure to be overtaken.'" (Surat ash-Shuara: 61)

As a matter of fact, this was neither the first nor the last time that the Children of Israel displayed such behaviour in which they showed no submission. The people of Musa had complained to him once before saying: "We have had (nothing but) trouble, both before and after thou camest to us." (Surat al-Araf: 129) Contrary to the weak conduct of his people, Musa was extremely confident, since he had profound trust in Allah. Right from the beginning of his struggle, Allah had informed him that His help and support would be with him: "Fear not: for I am with you: I hear and see (everything)." (Surah Ta-Ha: 46)

When Musa first met the sorcerers of Fir'awn, he felt "a sort of fear" (Surah Ta-Ha: 67). Thereupon, Allah revealed to him that he should not fear at all and that he would definitely overcome in the end. (Surah Ta-Ha: 68). Thus, Musa was educated by Allah and acquired a full maturity in respect to His ways. Consequently, when some of his people feared being overtaken, he said: "By no means! my Lord is with me! Soon will He guide me!" (Surat ash-Shuara: 62)

Allah revealed to Musa that he should strike the sea with his rod. Upon this, "it divided, and each separate part became like the huge, firm mass of a mountain." (Surat ash-Shuara: 63) In fact, at the moment when Fir'awn saw such a miracle, he should have understood that there was something extraordinary about the situation, and that he was seeing Divine intervention. The sea opened for the people whom Fir'awn wanted to destroy. Moreover, there was no guarantee that the sea would not close back after they passed across. Still, he and his army followed the Children of Israel into the sea. Most probably, Fir'awn and his soldiers had lost their ability to think reasonably because of their insolence and spite, and were unable comprehend the miraculous nature of the situation.

The Qur'an describes the last moments of Fir'awn as follows:

We took the Children of Israel across the sea: Fir'awn and his hosts followed them in insolence and spite. At length, when overwhelmed with the
flood, he said: "I believe that there is no god except Him Whom the Children of Israel believe in: I am of those who submit (to Allah in Islam)."
(Surah Yunus: 90)

Here, it is possible to see another miracle of Musa. Let us remind ourselves of the following verse:

Musa prayed: "Our Lord! Thou hast indeed bestowed on Fir'awn and his
chiefs splendour and wealth in the life of the present, and so, Our Lord,
they mislead (men) from Thy Path. Deface our Lord, the features of their
wealth, and send hardness to their hearts, so they will not believe until they
see the grievous penalty."
Allah said: "Accepted is your prayer (O Musa and Harun)! So stand ye
straight, and follow not the path of those who know not." (Surah Yunus:
88-89)

It is clearly understood from this verse that Musa was thus informed in
answer to his supplication that Fir'awn would believe in Allah at the time
he faced the painful punishment. Indeed, Fir'awn said that he believed in
Allah when the waters started to cover. Yet, it was very clear that his
behaviour was insincere and false. Fir'awn most probably said so to save
himself from dying.

Certainly, the last-moment acceptance of faith of Fir'awn and his asking
for forgiveness were not accepted by Allah. Fir'awn and his army could not
be saved from death by drowning.

(It was said to him): "Ah now! But a little while before, wast thou in rebellion! and thou didst mischief (and violence)! This day shall We save thee in
the body, that thou mayest be a sign to those who come after thee! But verily, many among mankind are heedless of Our Signs!" (Surah Yunus: 91-92)

We are also informed that his men, as well as Fir'awn himself, received
their share of the punishment. Since the soldiers of Fir'awn were men of
"insolence and spite" (Surah Yunus: 90), "men of sin" (Surat al-Qasas: 8),
"did wrong" (Surat al-Qasas: 40), and "thought that they would not have to
return to Allah" (Surat al-Qasas: 39) just like Fir'awn, they well deserved
the punishment of Allah. Thus, Allah seized both Fir'awn and his hosts and
flung them into the sea. (Surat al-Qasas: 40)

So Allah exacted retribution from them and drowned them in the sea, because they rejected His signs and failed to take warning from them. (Surat al-Araf: 136)

Allah describes in the Qur'an in the following verses, all that happened after the death of Fir'awn:

> And We made a people, considered weak (and of no account), inheritors of lands in both east and west - lands whereon We sent down Our blessings. The fair promise of thy Lord was fulfilled for the Children of Israel, because they had patience and constancy, and We levelled to the ground the great works and fine buildings which Fir'awn and his people erected (with such pride). (Surat al-Araf: 137)

Chapter 7

The People of Saba and the Arim Flood

There was, for Saba, aforetime, a Sign in their home-land - two Gardens to the right and to the left. "Eat of the Sustenance (provided) by your Lord, and be grateful to Him: a territory fair and happy, and a Lord Oft-Forgiving!" But they turned away (from Allah), and We sent against them the Flood (released) from the dams, and We converted their two garden (rows) into "gardens" producing bitter fruit, and tamarisks, and some few (stunted) Lote-trees.

(Surah Saba: 15-16)

T he community of Saba was one of the four biggest civilisations which lived in South Arabia. This people is estimated to have been established some time between 1000-750 BC and to have collapsed around 550 AD with the two centuries-long attacks of the Persians and the Arabs.

The date of the establishment of the civilisation of Saba is a subject of much discussion. The people of Saba started recording their governmental reports around 600 BC. This is why there are no records of them prior to this date.

The oldest sources which refer to the people of Saba are annual war chronicles left from the time of the Assyrian King Sargon II. (722-705 BC) While Sargon records about the people that pay taxes to him, he also refers to the King of Saba, Yith'i-amara (It'amara). This record is the oldest written source that yields information about the Saba civilisation. Yet, it would not be right to draw the conclusion that the Saba culture was established around 700 BC depending only on this source, for it is highly

probable that Saba had existed for quite some time before it was recorded in written records. This means that the history of Saba may predate the above. Indeed, in the inscriptions of Arad-Nannar, one of the latest kings of the state of Ur, the word "Sabum", which is thought to mean "the country of Saba", was used.[39] If this word does mean Saba, then, this shows that the history of Saba goes back as far as 2500 BC.

Historical sources telling about Saba usually say that this was a culture, like the Phoenicians, particularly involved in commercial activities. Accordingly, these people owned and administered some of the trade routes passing across Northern Arabia. In order for the Sabaean traders to carry their goods to the Mediterranean and Gaza, and thus pass across Northern Arabia, they had to get permission from Sargon II, the ruler of all the region, or pay a certain amount of tax to him. When the Sabaean people started paying taxes to the Assyrian Kingdom, their name began to be recorded in the annals of this state.

The Sabaeans are known to have been a civilised people in history. In the inscriptions of the rulers of Saba, words such as "restore", "dedicate" and "construct" are frequently used. The Ma'rib Dam, which is one of the most important monuments of this people, is an important indication of the technological level this people had reached. However, this did not mean that the military power of the Sabaeans was weak; the Sabaean army was one of the most important factors contributing to the endurance of their culture over such a long period without collapse.

The Sabaean state had one of the strongest armies in the region. The state was able to adopt an expansionist policy thanks to its army. The Sabaean state had conquered the lands of the Old Qataban state. It owned many lands on the African continent. During 24 BC, during an expedition to Magrib, the Sabaean army utterly defeated the army of Marcus Aelius Gallus, the Governor of Egypt for the Roman Empire which was definitely the strongest state at the time. Saba can be portrayed as a state that pursued moderate policies, yet did not hesitate to use power when necessary. With its advanced culture and army, the Sabaean state was definitely one of the "super powers" of the region at the time.

criptions written in
language of the
ple of Saba.

This extraordinarily strong army of the Sabaean state is also described .in the Qur'an. An expression of the commanders of the Saba army related in the Qur'an, shows the extent of the confidence this army had in itself. The commanders call out to the female ruler (queen) of the state: "We are endued with strength, and given to vehement war: but the command is with thee; so consider what thou wilt command." (Surat an-Naml: 33)

The capital city of the Sabaean state was Ma'rib, which was quite wealthy thanks to the advantageous position of its geography. The capital city was very close to the River Adhanah. The point where the river reached Jabal Balaq was very suitable for the construction of a dam. Making use of this condition, the Sabaean people constructed a dam at this location at the time when their civilisation was first established, and they began irrigation. They indeed reached a very high level of prosperity. The capital city, Ma'rib, was one of the most developed cities of the time. The Greek writer Pliny, who had visited the region and greatly praised it, also mentioned how green this region was.[40]

The height of the dam in Ma'rib was 16 metres, its width was 60 metres and its length was 620 metres. According to the calculations, the total area that could be irrigated by the dam was 9,600 hectares, of which 5,300 hectares belonged to the southern plain, while the remaining part belonged to the northern plain. These two plains were referred to as "Ma'rib and two plains" in the Sabaean inscriptions[41] . The expression in the Qur'an, "two gardens to the right and to the left", points to the imposing gardens and vineyards in these two valleys. Thanks to this dam and its irrigation systems, the region became famous as the best irrigated and most fruitful area of Yemen. The Frenchman J. Holevy and the Austrian Glaser proved from written documents that the Ma'rib dam existed since ancient times. In documents written in the Himer dialect, it is related that this dam rendered the territory very productive.

This dam was extensively repaired during the 5th and 6th centuries AD. Yet, these reparations could not prevent the dam from collapsing in 542 AD. The collapse of the dam resulted in the "flood of Arim" mentioned in the Qur'an which caused great damage. The vineyards, gardens and the cultivated fields of the Sabaean people, which they had cultivated for hundreds of years, were completely destroyed. It is also known that the Sabaean people quickly went into a period of recession after the destruction of the dam. The end of the Sabaean state came at the end of this period which had begun with the destruction of the dam.

With the Ma'rib Dam, which they had constructed with very advanced technology, the Sabaean people became owners of a great irrigation capacity. The fruitful lands they thus obtained and their control over the trade routes allowed them to lead a magnificent and luxurious lifestyle. However, they "turned away" from Allah to whom they should have been grateful for all those bounties mentioned above. Therefore, their dam collapsed and the "flood of Arim" destroyed all their attainments.

The Flood of Arim which was Sent to the State of Saba

When we examine the Qur'an in the light of the historical data above, we observe that there is very substantial agreement here. Archaeological findings and the historical data both verify what is recorded in the Qur'an. As mentioned in the verse, these people, who did not listen to the exhortations of their prophet and who ungratefully rejected faith, were in the end punished with a dreadful flood. This flood is described in the Qur'an in the following verses:

> There was, for Saba, aforetime, a Sign in their home-land - two Gardens to the right and to the left. "Eat of the Sustenance (provided) by your Lord, and be grateful to Him: a territory fair and happy, and a Lord Oft-Forgiving!" But they turned away (from Allah), and We sent against them the Flood (released) from the dams, and We converted their two garden (rows) into "gardens" producing bitter fruit, and tamarisks, and some few (stunted) Lote-trees. That was the Requital We gave them because they ungratefully rejected Faith: and never do We give (such) requital except to such as are ungrateful rejecters. (Surah Saba: 15-17)

As emphasised in the above verses, the Sabaean people were living in a region noted for its outstanding aesthetic, fruitful vineyards and gardens. Situated on the trade routes, the country of Saba had quite a high standard of living and was one of the most favoured cities of the time.

In such a country, where standards of living and circumstances were so positive, what the Sabaean people should have done was to "Eat of the Sustenance (provided) by their Lord, and be grateful to Him" as is said in the verse. Yet, they did not do so. They chose to lay claim to the prosperity they had. They thought that this country belonged to themselves, that it was they who made all these extraordinary circumstances possible. They chose to be arrogant instead of being grateful, and, in the expression of the verse, they "turned away from Allah"...

Because they laid claim to all the prosperity they had, they lost it all. As related in the verse, the flood of Arim destroyed everything they had.

In the Qur'an, the punishment sent to the Sabaean people is named as "Sayl al-Arim" which means the "flood of Arim". This expression used in

Today, the famous dam of the Sabaeans has been turned into irrigation facilities.

The Ma'rib Dam seen above in ruins was one of the most important works of the Sabaean people. This dam collapsed because of the flood of Arim mentioned in the Qur'an and all the cultivated areas were swamped. Its territory destroyed with the collapsing of the dam, the Sabaean state lost its economic strength in a very short time and was soon completely demolished.

the Qur'an also tells us the way this disaster occurred. The word "Arim" means dam or barrier. The expression of "Sayl al-Arim" describes a flood that came about with the collapse of this barrier. Islamic commentators have resolved the issue of time and place being guided by the terms used in the Qur'an about the flood of Arim. Mawdudi writes in his commentary:

As also used in the expression, Sayl al-Arim, the word "arim" is derived

The Qur'an tells us that the Queen of Saba and her people were "worshipping the sun besides Allah" before she followed Sulayman. The information on the inscriptions verify this fact and indicate that they were worshipping the sun and the moon in their temples, one of which is seen above.

On the pillars, there are inscriptions written in the Sabaean language.

from the word "arimen" used in the Southern Arabic dialect, which means "dam, barrier". In the ruins unearthed in the excavations made in Yemen, this word was seen to be frequently used in this meaning. For example, in the inscriptions which was ordered by Yemen's Habesh monarch, Ebrehe (Abraha), after the restoration of the big Ma'rib wall in 542 and 543 AD, this word was used to mean dam (barrier) time and again. So, the expression of Sayl al- Arim means "a flood disaster which occurs after the destruction of a dam."

"We converted their two garden (rows) into gardens producing bitter fruit, and tamarisks, and some few (stunted) Lote-trees" (Surah Saba: 16). That is, after the collapse of the dam-wall, all the country was inundated by the flood. The canals that had been dug by the Sabaean people, and the wall that had been constructed by building barriers between the mountains, were destroyed and the irrigation system fell apart. As a result, the territory, which was like a garden before, turned into a jungle. There was no fruit left but the cherry-like fruit of little stumpy trees.[42]

The Christian archaeologist Werner Keller, writer of "The Holy Book Was Right" *(Und Die Bible Hat Doch Recht)*, accepted that the flood of Arim occurred according to the description of the Qur'an and wrote that the existence of such a dam and the destruction of the whole country by its collapse proves that the example given in the Qur'an about the people of the garden was indeed realized.[43]

After the disaster of the Arim flood, the region started to turn into a desert and the Sabaean people lost their most important source of income with the disappearance of their agricultural lands. The people, who had not heeded the call of Allah to believe in Him and to be grateful to Him, were in the end punished with such a disaster as this. After the great destruction caused by the flood, the people started to disintegrate. The Sabaean people started to desert their houses and emigrate to Northern Arabia, Makkah and Syria.[44]

Since the flood took place after the composition of the Old and the New Testaments, this event is described only in the Qur'an.

The city of Ma'rib, which was once a residence for the Sabaean people, but is now only a desolate ruin, undoubtedly is a warning to those who repeat the same mistake as the Sabaean people. The Sabaean people were not the only people that were destroyed by a flood. In Surat al-Kahf of the Qur'an, the story of two garden owners is told. One of these men possesses a very imposing and productive garden like those of the Sabaean people. However, he makes the same mistake as them: turning away from Allah. He thinks that the favour bestowed on him "belongs" to him himself, i.e. he is the cause of it:

> Set forth to them the parable of two men: for one of them We provided two gardens of grape-vines and surrounded them with date palms; in between the two We placed corn-fields. Each of those gardens brought forth its produce, and failed not in the least therein: in the midst of them We caused a river to flow.
>
> (Abundant) was the produce this man had. He said to his companion, in the course of a mutual argument: "more wealth have I than you, and more honour and power in (my following of) men." He went into his garden in a state (of mind) unjust to his soul: He said, "I deem not that this will ever perish, Nor do I deem that the Hour (of Judgment) will (ever) come: Even if I am brought back to my Lord, I shall surely find (there) something better in exchange."
>
> His companion said to him, in the course of the argument with him: "Dost thou deny Him Who created thee out of dust, then out of a sperm-drop, then fashioned thee into a man? But (I think) for my part that He is Allah, My Lord, and none shall I associate with my Lord. Why didst thou not, as thou wentest into thy garden, say: 'Allah's will (be done)! There is no power but with Allah!' If thou dost see me less than thee in wealth and sons, It may be that my Lord will give me something better than thy garden, and that He will send on thy garden thunderbolts (by way of reckoning) from heaven, making it (but) slippery sand!- Or the water of the garden will run off underground so that thou wilt never be able to find it."
>
> So his fruits (and enjoyment) were encompassed (with ruin), and he remained twisting and turning his hands over what he had spent on his property, which had (now) tumbled to pieces to its very foundations, and he

could only say, "Woe is me! Would I had never ascribed partners to my Lord and Cherisher!" Nor had he numbers to help him against Allah, nor was he able to deliver himself. There, the (only) protection comes from Allah, the True One. He is the Best to reward, and the Best to give success. (Surat al-Kahf: 32-44)

As understood from the verses, the mistake of this garden owner was not to deny the existence of Allah. He does not deny the existence of Allah, on the contrary he supposed that "even if he is brought back to his Lord" he would certainly find something better in exchange. He held that the state he is in, was due to his own successful efforts.

Actually, this is exactly what associating partners to Allah means: attempting to lay claim to everything that belongs to Allah and losing one's fear of Allah thinking that one has some particular grace of his own, and Allah will somehow "show favour" to one.

This is what the Sabaean people also did. Their punishment was the same - all of their territory was destroyed - so that they could understand that they were not the ones who were the "owners" of power but that it was only "bestowed" on them...

Chapter 8

The Prophet Sulayman and the Queen of Saba

She was asked to enter the lofty Palace: but when she saw it, she tho-
ught it was a lake of water, and she (tucked up her skirts), uncovering
her legs. He said: "This is but a palace paved smooth with slabs of
glass." She said: "O my Lord! I have indeed wronged my soul: I do
(now) submit (in Islam), with Sulayman, to the Lord of the Worlds."
(Surat an-Naml: 44)

H istorical records regarding the meeting of Sulayman and the
Queen of Saba were brought into daylight by examinations
made in the old country of Saba in South Yemen. Examinations made on the ruins revealed that a "queen" lived in the region betwe-
en 1000 and 950 BC and travelled towards the north (to Jerusalem).

Details of what happened between these two rulers, the economical
and political power of their countries, their regimes and some other details are all explained in the Surat an-Naml. The story, which covers a large
part of Surat an-Naml, begins its reference to the Queen of Saba with the
news which the Hudhud (a Hoopoe bird), a member of Sulayman's army,
gives to Sulayman:

> But the Hoopoe tarried not far: he (came up and) said: "I have compassed
> (territory) which thou hast not compassed, and I have come to thee from
> Saba with tidings true. I found (there) a woman ruling over them and pro-
> vided with every requisite; and she has a magnificent throne.
> I found her and her people worshipping the sun besides Allah: Satan has
> made their deeds seem pleasing in their eyes, and has kept them away

from the Path -so they receive no guidance- (Kept them away from the Path), that they should not worship Allah, Who brings to light what is hidden in the heavens and the earth, and knows what ye hide and what ye reveal. Allah!- there is no god but He!- Lord of the Throne Supreme!" (Sulayman) said: "Soon shall we see whether thou hast told the truth or lied!" (Surat an-Naml: 22-27)

After receiving this news from the Hoopoe, Sulayman gave the following commands to him:

"Go thou, with this letter of mine, and deliver it to them: then draw back from them, and (wait to) see what answer they return" (Surat an-Naml: 28)

After this, the Qur'an tells about the events that developed after the Queen of Saba received the letter:

(The queen) said: "Ye chiefs! here is delivered to me - a letter worthy of respect. It is from Sulayman, and is (as follows): 'In the name of Allah, Most Gracious, Most Merciful: Be ye not arrogant against me, but come to me in submission (to the true Religion).'"
She said: "Ye chiefs! advise me in (this) my affair: no affair have I decided except in your presence."
They said: "We are endued with strength, and given to vehement war: but the command is with thee; so consider what thou wilt command." She said: "Kings, when they enter a country, despoil it, and make the noblest of its people its meanest thus do they behave. But I am going to send him a present, and (wait) to see with what (answer) return (my) ambassadors."
Now when (the embassy) came to Sulayman, he said: "Will ye give me abundance in wealth? But that which Allah has given me is better than that which He has given you! Nay it is ye who rejoice in your gift! Go back to them, and be sure we shall come to them with such hosts as they will never be able to meet: We shall expel them from there in disgrace, and they will feel humbled (indeed)."
He said (to his own men): "Ye chiefs! which of you can bring me her throne before they come to me in submission?" Said an 'Ifrit, of the Jinns: "I will bring it to thee before thou rise from thy council: indeed I have full strength for the purpose, and may be trusted."
Said one who had knowledge of the Book: "I will bring it to thee within the twinkling of an eye!" Then when (Sulayman) saw it placed firmly before him, he said: "This is by the Grace of my Lord!- to test me whether I am grateful or ungrateful! and if any is grateful, truly his gratitude is (a gain)

for his own soul; but if any is ungrateful, truly my Lord is Free of all Needs, Supreme in Honour !"

He said: "Transform her throne out of all recognition by her: let us see whether she is guided (to the truth) or is one of those who receive no guidance."

So when she arrived, she was asked, "Is this thy throne?" She said, "It was just like this; and knowledge was bestowed on us in advance of this, and we have submitted to Allah (in Islam)." And he diverted her from the worship of others besides Allah: for she was (sprung) of a people that had no faith. She was asked to enter the lofty Palace: but when she saw it, she thought it was a lake of water, and she (tucked up her skirts), uncovering her legs. He said: "This is but a palace paved smooth with slabs of glass." She said: "O my Lord! I have indeed wronged my soul: I do (now) submit (in Islam), with Sulayman, to the Lord of the Worlds." (Surat an-Naml: 29-44)

The queen of Saba was very impressed when she saw Sulayman's palace and she submitted in Islam with Sulayman.

A map showing the two-way route of the queen of Saba.

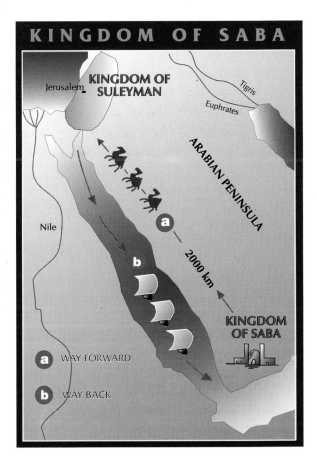

KINGDOM OF SABA

KINGDOM OF SULEYMAN

Jerusalem

Tigris

Euphrates

ARABIAN PENINSULA

Nile

2000 km

KINGDOM OF SABA

a WAY FORWARD

b WAY BACK

Sulayman's Palace

In the chapters and verses that refer to the Queen of Saba, the prophet Sulayman is also mentioned. While it is told in the Qur'an that he has a magnificent palace and kingdom, many other details are also given.

According to these, Sulayman had the most advanced technology of his day. In his palace were striking pieces of art and other valuable objects, which impressed all those who saw them. The entrance of the palace was made of glass. The Qur'an describes this palace and its effects on the Queen of Saba in the following verses:

She was asked to enter the lofty Palace: but when she saw it, she thought it was a lake of water, and she (tucked up her skirts), uncovering her legs. He said: "This is but a palace paved smooth with slabs of glass." She said: "O my Lord! I have indeed wronged my soul: I do (now) submit (in Islam), with Sulayman, to the Lord of the Worlds." (Surat an-Naml: 44)

Prophet Sulayman's palace is called "Solomon's Temple" in Jewish literature. Today, only the "Western Wall" of the so called temple or palace stands and this is at the same time, the place named "The Wailing Wall" by the Jews. The reason why this palace as well as many other places in Jerusalem were later demolished, is because of the mischievous and arrogant conduct of subsequent Jews. The Qur'an informs us about this as follows:

And We gave (Clear) Warning to the Children of Israel in the Book, that twice would they do mischief on the earth and be elated with mighty arrogance (and twice would they be punished)! When the first of the warnings came to pass, We sent against you Our servants given to terrible warfare: They entered the very inmost parts of your homes; and it was a warning (completely) fulfilled.

Then did We grant you the Return as against them: We gave you increase in resources and sons, and made you the more numerous in man-power. If ye did well, ye did well for yourselves; if ye did evil, (ye did it) against yourselves. So when the second of the warnings came to pass, (We permitted your enemies) to disfigure your faces, and to enter your Temple as they had entered it before, and to visit with destruction all that fell into their power. (Surat al-Isra: 4-7)

Sulayman's Temple

After Solomon's Temple was destroyed, the only wall of the temple that remained was turned into the "Wailing Wall" by the Jews. After conquering Jerusalem during the 7th century, the Muslims built the Mosque of 'Umar and the Dome of the Rock where the temple once stood. Jerusalem still retains this. In the picture at the right is seen Dome of the Rock.

Solomon's Temple had the most advanced technology of the time and a superior understanding of aesthetics. In the upper plan is shown the center of Jerusalem during the prophet Sulayman's reign. 1) Southwest door 2) Queen's palace 3) Sulayman's palace 4) Entrance with 32 pillars 5) Law court 6) The Forest of Lebanon 7) The house of the high priests 8) The entrance of the Temple 9) The courtyard of the Temple 10) The temple

All the people described in the previous chapters deserved punishment because of their rebellion and ingratitude for Allah's favours, and therefore they suffered disaster. Having wandered from one place to another for centuries without any country or state, and finally finding a home in the holy lands at the time of Sulayman, the Jews were again destroyed because of their transgression beyond all bounds, and because of their corruption and disobedience. Modern Jews, who have settled in the same region in the recent past, are again causing corruption and are "elated with mighty arrogance", just as they did before the first warning.

Chapter 9

Companions of the Cave

Or dost thou reflect that the Companions of
the Cave and of the Inscription were won-
ders among Our Sign? (Surat al-Kahf: 9)

T he Qur'an's 18th Surah named "Al-Kahf", meaning "the cave",
tells about a group of young people who took shelter in a cave
to hide away from a ruler who denied Allah and practised oppression and injustice upon the believers. The verses on the subject are as
follows:

Or dost thou reflect that the Companions of the Cave and of the Inscription were wonders among Our Sign?

Behold, the youths betook themselves to the Cave: they said, "Our Lord!
bestow on us Mercy from Thyself, and dispose of our affair for us in the
right way!"

Then We draw (a veil) over their ears, for a number of years, in the Cave,
(so that they heard not):

Then We roused them, in order to test which of the two parties was best
at calculating the term of years they had tarried!

We relate to thee their story in truth: they were youths who believed in their Lord, and We advanced them in guidance:

We gave strength to their hearts: Behold, they stood up and said: "Our Lord
is the Lord of the heavens and of the earth: never shall we call upon any
god other than Him: if we did, we should indeed have uttered an enormity!
These our people have taken for worship gods other than Him: why do
they not bring forward an authority clear (and convincing) for what they
do? Who doth more wrong than such as invent a falsehood against Allah?"

"When ye turn away from them and the things they worship other than Allah, betake yourselves to the Cave: Your Lord will shower His mercies on you and disposes of your affair towards comfort and ease."

Thou wouldst have seen the sun, when it rose, declining to the right from their Cave, and when it set, turning away from them to the left, while they lay in the open space in the midst of the Cave. Such are among the Signs of Allah: He whom Allah, guides is rightly guided; but he whom Allah leaves to stray -for him wilt thou find no protector to lead him to the Right Way.

Thou wouldst have deemed them awake, whilst they were asleep, and We turned them on their right and on their left sides: their dog stretching forth his two fore-legs on the threshold: if thou hadst come up on to them, thou wouldst have certainly turned back from them in flight, and wouldst certainly have been filled with terror of them.

Such (being their state), we raised them up (from sleep), that they might question each other. Said one of them, "How long have ye stayed (here)?" They said, "We have stayed (perhaps) a day, or part of a day. (At length)" they (all) said, "Allah (alone) knows best how long ye have stayed here? Now send ye then one of you with this money of yours to the town: let him find out which is the best food (to be had) and bring some to you, that (ye may) satisfy your hunger therewith: And let him behave with care and courtesy, and let him not inform any one about you.

For if they should come upon you, they would stone you or force you to return to their cult, and in that case ye would never attain prosperity.""

Thus did We make their case known to the people, that they might know that the promise of Allah is true, and that there can be no doubt about the Hour of Judgment. Behold, they dispute among themselves as to their affair. (Some) said, "Construct a building over them": Their Lord knows best about them: those who prevailed over their affair said, "Let us surely build a place of worship over them."

(Some) say they were three, the dog being the fourth among them; (others) say they were five, the dog being the sixth -doubtfully guessing at the unknown; (yet others) say they were seven, the dog being the eighth.

Say thou: "My Lord knoweth best their number; It is but few that know their (real case)." Enter not, therefore, into controversies concerning them, except on a matter that is clear, nor consult any of them about (the affair of) the Sleepers.

Nor say of anything, "I shall be sure to do so and so tomorrow"- without adding, "So please Allah!" and call thy Lord to mind when thou forgettest, and say, "I hope that my Lord will guide me ever closer (even) than this to the right road."

So they stayed in their Cave three hundred years, and (some) add nine (more) Say: "Allah knows best how long they stayed: with Him is (the knowledge of) the secrets of the heavens and the earth: how clearly He sees, how finely He hears (everything)! They have no protector other than Him; nor does He share His Command with any person whatsoever." (Surat al-Kahf: 9-26)

According to widespread belief, the Companions of the Cave who are praised both by the Islamic and Christian sources, were subjected to the cruel tyranny of the Roman Emperor, Decius. Meeting the oppression and injustice of Decius, these young people warned their own people many times not to abandon the religion of Allah. The indifference of their people to their communication of the message, the increase in oppression of the emperor and their being threatened with death, caused them to leave their homes.

As historical documents verify, at that time, many emperors extensively executed policies of terror, oppression, and injustice on believers who stood for early Christianity in its original and pure form.

In a letter written by the Roman Governor Pilinius (69-113 AD) who was in North West Anatolia, to the Emperor Trayanus, he referred to "the companions of the Messiah (the Christians) who were punished because they resisted worshipping the statue of the Emperor." This letter is one of the important documents which relate the oppression visited on early Christians at that time. Under such circumstances, these young people, who were asked to submit to a non-religionist system and to worship an emperor as a god apart from Allah, did not accept this and said;

"Our Lord is the Lord of the heavens and of the earth: never shall we call upon any god other than Him: if we did, we should indeed have uttered an enormity! These our people have taken for worship gods other than Him: why do they not bring forward an authority clear (and convincing) for what they do? Who doth more wrong than such as invent a falsehood against Allah?" (Surat al-Kahf: 14-15)

As regards the region where the Companions of the Cave lived, there are several different opinions. The most reasonable of these are Ephesus and Tarsus.

Almost all the Christian sources show Ephesus as the location of the Cave where these young believers took shelter. Some Muslim researchers and the Qur'anic commentators agree with the Christians regarding Ephesus. Some others, explained in detail that Ephesus was not the place, and then tried to prove that the event took place in Tarsus. In this study, both of these alternatives will be dealt with. Yet, all those researchers and commentators - including the Christians - said that the event took place at the time of Roman Emperor Decius (also called as Decianus), around 250 AD.

Decius, together with Nero, is known to be the Roman Emperor, who most severely tortured the Christians. During his short reign, he passed a law that compelled everyone under his rule to offer a sacrifice to the Roman gods. Everyone was obliged to offer a sacrifice to these deities, and moreover, to get a certificate showing that they had done this, which they had to show to state officials. Those who did not obey were executed. In Christian sources, it is written that a great majority of the Christians refused this idolatrous act and fled from "one city to another", or hid in secret shelters. The Companions of the Cave are most probably a group among these early Christians.

Meanwhile, there is a point that has to be emphasised here: this topic has been narrated in a story-like manner by some of Muslim and Christian historians and commentators, and turned into a legend as a result of the addition of much falsehood and hearsay. However, this incident is a historical reality.

Are the Companions of the Cave in Ephesus?

As regards the city where these young people lived and the cave in which they took shelter, various places are indicated in different sources. The main reasons for this are: people's wish to believe that such courageous and brave-hearted people lived in their town, and the great similarity of the caves in those regions. For instance, in almost all of these places, there is a place of worship said to be built over caves.

As is well known, Ephesus was accepted to be a holy place by the Christians, because, there is a house in this city which was said to be the Virgin Mary's and which was later turned into a church. So, it is highly probable that the Companions of the Cave resided in one of those holy places. Moreover, some Christian sources state their certainty that it was the place.

The oldest source on the subject is the Syrian priest, James of Saruc (born 452 AD). The famous historian, Gibbon, has taken many quotations from James' study, in his book *The Decline and Fall of the Roman Empire.* According to this book, the name of the Emperor, who tortured the seven young Christian believers and compelled them to hide away in a cave, was Decius. Decius ruled over the Roman Empire between 249-251 AD and his period of reign is widely known for the torments he practised on the followers of 'Isa (Jesus). According to Muslim commentators, the region where the event took place was either "Aphesus" or "Aphesos". According to Gibbon, the name of this place is Ephesus. Situated on the western coast of Anatolia, this city was one of the largest ports and cities of the Roman Empire. The ruins of this city are known as "The Antique City of Ephesus" today.

The name of the Emperor who reigned in the period when the Companions of the Cave woke up from their long sleep, is Tezusius according to Muslim researchers, whereas it is Theodosius II according to Gibbons. This Emperor ruled between 408-450 AD, after the Roman Empire had converted to Christianity.

Referring to the verse below, in some commentaries it is said that the entrance of the cave looks towards the north, and hence the sunlight could not penetrate inside. Thus, someone passing by the cave could not see what was inside at all. The related verse of the Qur'an informs:

> Thou wouldst have seen the sun, when it rose, declining to the right from their Cave, and when it set, turning away from them to the left, while they lay in the open space in the midst of the Cave. Such are among the Signs of Allah: He whom Allah, guides is rightly guided; but he whom Allah leaves to stray,- for him wilt thou find no protector to lead him to the Right Way. (Surat al-Kahf: 17)

The interior of
the Cave in
Ephesus which
is thought to be
the one of the
Companions of
the Cave.

The cave in Ephesus seen from the outside.

The archaeologist Dr. Musa Baran points to Ephesus as the place where this group of young believers lived, in his book named *Ephesus*, and he adds:

> In the year 250 BC, seven young people living in Ephesus choose Christianity and reject idolatry. Trying to find a way out, these young people find a cave in the eastern slope of the Pion mountain. The Roman soldiers see this and build a wall to the entrance of the cave. [45]

Today, it is acknowledged that over these old ruins and graves, many religious constructions are built. Excavations made by the Austrian Archaeological Institute in 1926, revealed that the ruins found on the eastern slope of the Pion mountain belonged to a construction built on behalf of the Companions of the Cave in the middle of the 7th century (during the rule of Theodosius II). [46]

Are the Companions of the Cave in Tarsus?

The second place presented as the place where the Companions of the Cave have lived, is Tarsus. Indeed, there is a cave that is very similar to the one described in the Qur'an, which is located on a mountain known either as Encilus or Bencilus, to the north-west of Tarsus.

The idea that Tarsus is the correct location is the view of many Islamic scholars. One of the most important Qur'anic interpreters, at-Tabari specifi-

The cave in Tarsus that is thought to belong to the Companions of the Cave.

ed the name of the mountain where the cave stood as "Bencilus" in his book named *Tarikh al-Umam*, and added that this mountain was in Tarsus. [47]

Again, another famous commentator on the Qur'an, Muhammed Emin stated that the name of the mountain was "Pencilus" and that it was in Tarsus. The name that is pronounced as "Pencilus" may sometimes be pronounced as "Encilus". According to him, the difference between the words is caused by different pronunciations of the letter "B" or by the loss of a letter from the original word which is called "historical word abrasion". [48]

Fakhruddin ar-Razi, another well known Qur'anic scholar, explains in his work that "even though this place is called Ephesus, the basic intention is to say Tarsus here, because Ephesus is just another name of Tarsus". [49]

In addition, in the commentaries of Qadi al-Baidawi and an-Nasafi, in the commentaries of al-Jalalayn and in at-Tibyan, in the commentaries of Elmali and O.Nasuhi Bilmen, and many other scholars, this place is specified as "Tarsus". Besides, all of these commentators explain the sentence of the 17th verse, "the sun, when it rose declined to the right from their cave, and when it set, turned away from them to the left", by saying that the mouth of the cave in the mountain looked towards the north. [50]

The residence of the Companions of the Cave was a subject of interest also at the time of the Ottoman Empire and some research was made on the subject. There is some correspondence and an exchange of information on the subject in the Ottoman Archives of the Prime Ministry. For instance, in a letter sent to the Treasury Superior of the Ottoman State by the local administration of Tarsus, there is a formal request and an attached message notifying of their demand to give salary to those people who dealt with the cleaning and maintenance of the cave of Ashab-ı Kahf (Companions of the Cave). The reply to this letter stated that in order for these salaries to be paid to the workers from the state treasury, it was necessary to find out whether this was indeed the place where the Companions of the Cave had resided. The research made for this purpose has been very useful in determining the real location of the Cave.

In a report prepared after an investigation made by the National Council, it was stated: "To the north of Tarsus, a province of Adana, there is a cave on a mountain two hours away from Tarsus, and the mouth of this cave looks to the north as stated in the Qur'an." [51]

The debates which developed as to who the Companions of the Cave were, where and when they lived, always led the authorities to make research into the subject and many comments were made on the subject. Yet, none of these comments may be considered certain, and, therefore, questions such as: at which period these young believers lived, and where the cave mentioned in the verses was, remain without substantial answers.

Conclusion

Do they not travel through the earth, and see what was the end of those before them? They were superior to them in strength: they tilled the soil and populated it in greater numbers than these have done: there came to them their messengers with Clear (Signs). (Which they rejected, to their own destruction): It was not Allah Who wronged them, but they wronged their own souls. (Surat ar-Room: 9)

All the peoples we have reviewed until now, had some qualities in common such as: transgressing against Allah, associating partners with Him, behaving arrogantly in the land, wrongfully devouring other's property, tending to sexual perversion, and insolence. Another common feature they had was their oppression and iniquity towards the Muslims in their vicinity. They tried in every way to intimidate the Muslims.

The purpose of the warnings of the Qur'an is surely not just to give history lessons. The Qur'an states that the stories of the prophets are told only to set an "example". Those nations who were earlier destroyed, should lead those who come after them to the right way:

Is it not a warning to such men (to call to mind) how many generations before them We destroyed, in whose haunts they (now) move? Verily, in this are Signs for men endued with understanding. (Surah Ta-Ha: 128)

If we consider all of these to be "examples", then we can see that some parts of our society are no better, in terms of degeneration and transgression, than the peoples who perished and which are described in these stories.

For example, most societies in our day have a high population of sodomists and homosexuals within them which remind us of the "People of Lut". The homosexuals, attending sex parties with "leading people of the society", display all kinds of perversions outdoing their counterparts in Sodom and Gomorrah. Especially, there are a group of them living in the largest cities of the world, who have "gone even further" than those in Pompeii.

All the societies we have examined have been punished through natural disasters such as earthquakes, storms, flood etc. Similarly, the societies that go astray and dare to commit the offences of past peoples may well be punished in a like manner.

It should not be forgotten that Allah may punish whatever person or nation He wills whenever He wills. Or, He may let whomever He wills lead a ordinary life in this world, and punish him in the Hereafter. The Qur'an states:

> Each one of them We seized for his crime: of them, against some We sent a violent tornado (with showers of stones); some were caught by a (mighty) Blast; some We caused the earth to swallow up; and some We drowned (in the waters): It was not Allah Who injured (or oppressed) them. They injured (and oppressed) their own souls. (Surat al-Ankaboot: 40)

The Qur'an also tells about a believer, who was from the family of Fir'awn and lived during the period of Musa, but who concealed his belief. He said to his people:

> "O my people! Truly I do fear for you something like the Day (of disaster) of the Confederates (in sin)!- Something like the fate of the People of Nuh, the 'Ad, and the Thamud, and those who came after them: but Allah never wishes injustice to his Servants.

> And O my people! I fear for you a Day when there will be Mutual calling (and wailing) - "A Day when ye shall turn your backs and flee: No defender shall ye have from Allah: Any whom Allah leaves to stray, there is none to guide..." (Surat al-Ghafir: 30-33)

All of the prophets warned their people, pointed out to them the Day of Judgement and attempted to make them frightened of Allah's punishment, just as did this believer who concealed his faith. The lives of all the prophets and messengers were passed in explaining these matters to their people over and over again. Yet most often, the people to whom they were sent accused them of untruthfulness, of seeking to acquire material gains, or trying to assert their superiority over them and then they went on to practise their own systems without thinking of what the prophet said or without questioning their deeds. Some of them have gone further and attempted to kill or drive away the believers. The number of the believers that obeyed and followed was often very few. However, in the cases of the rebellious communities, Allah always saved only the prophets and their followers.

Despite the thousands of years that have gone by, and the changes in places, manners, technologies and civilisations, yet not much has changed in the aforementioned social structures and the systems of the unbelievers. As we have emphasised above, a certain part of the society in which we live has all the corrupt qualities of the people described in the Qur'an. Just like Thamud who gave short measure, there are also a great number of forgers and swindlers today. There exists a "homosexual community", which is defended whenever the occasion shows itself, and the members of which do not fall short of the people of Lut in whom sexual perversion had reached its peak. A great part of society is made up of people as ungrateful and rebellious as Saba, as unthankful for the wealth endowed to them as the people of Iram, as unsubmissive and insulting towards the believers as the people of Nuh, and as heedless of social justice as ʿAd.

These are very significant signs...

We should always bear in mind that whatever differences come about in societies or at whatever stage of technological advancement they are or whatever their potentials are, that these have no importance whatsoever. None of these can save one from Allah's punishment. The Qur'an reminds us all of this reality:

Do they not travel through the earth, and see what was the end of those before them? They were superior to them in strength: they tilled the soil and populated it in greater numbers than these have done: there came to them their messengers with Clear (Signs). (Which they rejected, to their own destruction): It was not Allah Who wronged them, but they wronged their own souls. (Surat ar-Room: 9)

Glory to Thee, of knowledge We have none, save what Thou Hast taught us: In truth it is Thou Who art perfect in knowledge and wisdom. (Surat al-Baqara, 32)

Notes

Max Mallowan, *Nuh's Flood Reconsidered*, Iraq: XXVI-2, 1964, p.66

Ibid.

Muazzez Ilmiye Cig, *Kuran, Incil ve Tevrat'in Sümer'deki Kökleri*, 2.b., Istanbul: Kaynak, 1996

Werner Keller, *Und die Bibel hat doch recht* (The Bible as History; a Confirmation of the Book of Books), New York: William Morrow, 1964, pp. 25-29

Max Mallowan, *Nuh's Flood Reconsidered*, Iraq: XXVI-2, 1964, p. 70

Werner Keller, *Und die Bibel hat doch recht* (The Bible as History; a Confirmation of the Book of Books), New York: William Morrow, 1964, pp. 23-32

"Kish", *Britannica Micropaedia*, Volume 6, p. 893

"Shuruppak", *Britannica Micropaedia*, Volume 10, p. 772

Max Mallowan, *Early Dynastic Period in Mesopotamia*, Cambridge Ancient History 1-2, Cambridge: 1971, p. 238

0 Joseph Campbell, *Eastern Mythology*, p. 129

.1 *Bilim ve Utopya*, July 1996, 176. Footnote p. 19

2 Everett C. Blake, Anna G. Edmonds, *Biblical Sites in Turkey*, Istanbul: Redhouse Press, 1977, p. 13

3 Werner Keller, *Und die Bibel hat doch recht* (The Bible as History; a Confirmation of the Book of Books), New York: William Morrow, 1964 p. 75-76

.4 "Le Monde de la Bible", *Archeologie et Histoire*, July-August 1993.

.5 Werner Keller, *Und die Bibel hat doch recht* (The Bible as History; a Confirmation of the Book of Books), New York: William Morrow, 1964, p. 76

.6 Ibid, pp. 73-74

.7 Ibid, pp. 75-76

.8 G. Ernest Wright, "Bringing Old Testament Times to Life", *National Geographic*, Vol. 112, December 1957, p. 833

.9 Thomas H. Maugh II, "Ubar, Fabled Lost City, Found by LA Team", *The Los Angeles Times*, 5 February 1992.

.0 Kamal Salibi, *A History of Arabia*, Caravan Books, 1980

.1 Bertram Thomas, *Arabia Felix: Across the "Empty Quarter" of Arabia*, New York: Schrieber's Sons 1932, p. 161

.2 Charlene Crabb, "Frankincense", *Discover*, January 1993

.3 Nigel Groom, *Frankincense and Myrrh*, Longman, 1981, p. 81

.4 Ibid., p. 72

.5 Joachim Chwaszcza, *Yemen*, 4PA Press, 1992

.6 Ibid.

.7 Brian Doe, *Southern Arabia*, Thames and Hudson, 1971, p. 21

.8 Ça M'Interesse, January 1993

.9 "Hicr", Islam Ansiklopedisi: *Islam Alemi, Tarihi, Cografya, Etnografya ve Bibliyografya Lugati*, (Encyclopedia of Islam: Islamic World, History, Geography, Ethnography, and Bibliography Dictionary) Vol. 5/1, p. 475

30 Philip Hitti, *A History of the Arabs*, London: Macmillan, 1979, p. 37

31 "Thamuds", *Britannica Micropaedia*, Vol. 11, p. 672

32 Brian Doe, Southern Arabia, Thames and Hudson, 1971, pp. 21-22

33 Ernst H. Gombrich, *Gençler için Kisa Bir Dünya Tarihi*, (Translated into Turkish by Ahmet Mumcu from the German original script, Eine Kurze Weltgeschichte Für Junge Leser, Dumont Buchverlag, Köln, 1985), Istanbul: Inkilap Publishing House, 1997, p.25

34 Ernst H. Gombrich, *The Story of Art*, London MCML, The Phaidon Press Ltd., p. 42

35 Eli Barnavi, *Historical Atlas of The Jewish People*, London: Hutchinson, 1992, p. 4; "Egypt", *Encyclopedia Judaica*, Vol. 6, p. 481 and "The Exodus and Wanderings in Sinai", Vol. 8, p. 575; *Le Monde de la Bible*, No:83, July-August 1983, p. 50; *Le Monde de la Bible*, No:102, January-February 1997, pp. 29-32; Edward F. Wente, *The Oriental Institute News and Notes*, No:144, Winter 1995; Jacques Legrand, *Chronicle of The World*, Paris: Longman Chronicle, SA International Publishing, 1989, p. 68; David Ben Gurion, *A Historical Atlas Of the Jewish People*, New York: Windfall Book, 1974, p. 32

36 http: // www2.plaguescape.com /a/plaguescape/

37 "Red Sea", *Encyclopedia Judaica*, Volume 14, pp.14-15

38 David Ben-Gurion, *The Jews in Their Land*, New York: A Windfall Book, 1974, pp.32-33

39 "Seba" Islam Ansiklopedisi: *Islam Alemi, Tarihi, Cografya, Etnografya ve Bibliyografya Lugati*, (Encyclopedia of Islam: Islamic World, History, Geography, Ethnography, and Bibliography Dictionary) Vol.10, p. 268

40 Hommel, *Explorations in Bible Lands*, Philadelphia: 1903, p.739

41 "Marib", *Islam Ansiklopedisi: İslam Alemi, Tarihi, Coğrafya, Etnoğrafya ve Bibliyografya Lugatı*, Volume 7, p. 323-339.

42 Mawdudi, *Tefhimul Kuran*, Cilt 4, Istanbul: Insan Yayinlari, p.517.

43 Werner Keller, *Und die Bibel hat doch recht* (The Bible as History; a Confirmation of the Book of Books), New York: William Morrow, 1956, p.207.

44 *New Traveller's Guide to Yemen*, p.43.

45 Musa Baran, *Efes*, pp.23-24.

46 L.Massignon, *Opera Minora*, v.III, pp.104-108.

47 At-Tabari, Tarikh-al Umam.

48 Muhammed Emin.

49 Fakhruddin ar-Razi.

50 From the commentaries of Qadi al-Baidawi, an-Nasafi, al-Jalalayn and at-Tibyan, also Elmalili, Nasuhi Bilmen.

51 Ahmet Akgündüz, *Tarsus ve Tarihi ve Ashab-i Kehf.* (Tarsus and History and the Companions of the Cave.)

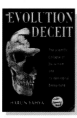

The Evolution Deceit has been published in many languages and created a sweeping effect across the world. The purpose of the book is to display the basic scientific facts that disprove the theory of evolution in every field and to make people aware of the inner truth, background and real purpose of this scientific fraud. The book is available in Russian, Turkish, Bosnian, Italian, Malay, Spanish, Indonesian, German and Albanian.

One of the purposes why the Qur'an was revealed is to summon people to think about creation and its works. When a person examines his own body or any other living thing in nature, the world or the whole universe, in it he sees a great design, art, plan and intelligence. All this is evidence proving God's being, unit, and eternal power. *For Men of Understanding* was written to make the reader see and realise some of the evidence of creation in nature. Many living miracles are revealed in the book with hundreds of pictures and brief explanations. *For Men of Understanding* is also available in Russian, German, French and urdu.